Ayurvedic Medicine for Dogs

Diane Morgan

FINDHORN PRESS

First published by Findhorn Press 2007

ISBN: 978-1-84409-125-6

British Library Cataloguing-in-Publication Data.
A catalogue record for this book is available from the British Library.

Edited by Jane Engel
Cover design by Damian Keenan
Layout by Pam Bochel
Printed and bound in the USA

1 2 3 4 5 6 7 8 9 10 11 12 13 12 11 10 09 08 07

Published by
Findhorn Press
305A The Park,
Findhorn, Forres
Scotland IV36 3TE

Tel 01309 690582
Fax 01309 690036
email: info@findhornpress.com
www.findhornpress.com

Contents

Chapter 1

Your Pet is the Universe

Your pet is the universe. What a statement. It seems, on the face of it, to be an extravagant, even a ridiculous claim. However, it's based solidly in both spiritual and physical fact. The "universe" is not simply some immensely large, amorphous "something" floating around in empty space. The universe is not only the stars and planets and space and time, but your table, your garden, your underwear, and your dog. It's a fabric that cannot tear, but which stretches infinitely to include and embrace all entities.

This brotherhood of being is the basis of Ayurvedic medicine. According to the National Institutes of Health's National Center for Complementary and Alternative Medicine, Ayurveda "aims to integrate and balance the body, mind, and spirit." And while Ayurveda is being rediscovered as a medical therapy, its primary concern has always been spiritual. One of the most honored of all ancient Ayurvedic texts, the Charaka Samhita (written about 500 B.C.) explains that the Ayurvedic physician must tend to the soul as well as to the spirit of the patient. Indeed, Ayurveda makes no hard and fast distinction between the physical, mental, and spiritual realms, a holistic concept that is just recently taking hold in Western medicine.

However, while talking about spirituality in human medicine (which is once again being given serious consideration), most physicians would stop short of acknowledging the spiritual dimension of animals. Ayurveda does not, which is one reason why it emphasizes a vegetarian diet for people. It understands not only that animals themselves have a spiritual dimension, but also that a spiritual bond exists between animals and humans, something we pet owners

The word "Ayurveda" is often translated "science of life," although a more accurate rendition might be "knowledge (veda) of life (ayur)."

have known all along. You are your dog's spiritual friend. This means that your kindness and love serve as a model for your dog's own karmic development. The fact that dogs are not sufficiently self-aware to understand karma and its role makes your help and love even more essential to his spiritual well being.

Life Is Easy and So Is Ayurveda

You may have heard otherwise. But believe it or not, although Ayurveda is based on some pretty complex theory, its actual practice is absolutely simple, down to earth, and easy to do. You don't have to learn Sanskrit, contort yourself (or worse contort your pet) into weird shapes, mumble mantras (although it helps), or achieve liberation to use Ayurveda to help your pet get well and stay well right now.

The following material gives the history and background of the Ayurvedic philosophy of life. If you are the more pragmatic sort, you can skip the rest of this chapter; however, a true understanding of how Ayurveda works depends upon knowing its basic principles.

Ayurveda, Philosophy, Science, and Medicine

It's all one!

The basic principles of Ayurvedic medicine are drawn from the Hindu tradition, the world's oldest global faith. It's also a faith that bears some eerie similarities to the most recent discoveries in physics. To top things off, it's only common sense. One difference between the origins of Ayurvedic and modern science is that Ayurveda is primarily deductive, which means it starts with a grand theory to explain the universe and works down from there. Most science is inductive, and begins with examination and observation of particular phenomena and works up from there. These two strategies are not competing, but complementary. True understanding depends on both.

Because of its holistic view, Ayurvedic medicine is goal oriented therapy that incorporates all sorts of different methodologies: surgery, herbs, massage, gems, color, diet, yoga, music and mantras, and other strategies. However, it also subsumes all modalities into its single, comprehensive world-view, and so it is a guided therapy, not a philosophical mish-mash of competing healing strategies. This is one aspect of Ayurveda that makes it different from western medicine, which focuses on the disease rather than the person having the disease. Western medicine has become so overspecialized that many western-trained veterinarians have problems seeing the whole picture, which includes the environment the animal lives in, and his critically important relationship with his owner. However, the techniques of western medicine also have a place in Ayurveda, especially in trauma care and acute conditions. Ayurvedic medicine, is, above all, about inclusiveness.

The Early Days

Ayurvedic medicine is the oldest systematized medical therapy in the world, going back at least 5000 years. It predates and is the basis for its better known cousin, Chinese medicine (and probably arrived there via the Silk Road). However, Ayurvedic medicine is based upon both spiritual and physical principles that are glossed over or ignored in Chinese medicine, which mostly confines itself to the analysis of Qi, the fundamental energy force that flows through all living things. Ayurvedic medicine is deeper and broader, and is as much concerned with spirit and mind as with body.

When the great Buddhist emperor Ashoka expanded his empire, Ayurvedic practice went with it. Buddhist monks planted Ayurvedic herb gardens throughout the Indian sphere of influence, and its basic principles spread not only to China but also to Sir Lanka, Nepal, Tibet, Mongolia, Russia, Korea, and Japan. Eventually Egypt, Greece, and Rome came to embrace Ayurvedic ideas. It is said that Alexander the Great relied upon Indian physicians to treat his soldiers for the numerous snakes bites they received. Greece doesn't have many poisonous snakes – certainly none to compare to cobras for deadliness. As for the Romans, those top predators and consumers of the ancient world bought so many Indian herbal products that the Roman historian Pliny the Younger complained about how much empire gold was being drained away.

As is true with all sacred Hindu knowledge, the earliest Ayurvedic masters handed down their knowledge orally to their disciples. Basic theory can be found in a subtext or "upa-Veda" of the Yajur-Veda, one of the holiest Vedic texts. Some theorists believe the origin can be found in the Rig-Veda, which is older and even holier; however, the heart of the Rig-Veda is a collection of hymns and any medical knowledge it contains is more metaphorical than technical.

Only in the fifth and sixth centuries B.C. was the full material committed to writing through the work of three scholars: Charaka, Sushruta, and Vagbhata. Their remarks are still worthwhile today. Charaka is said to have been the first physician anywhere to identify and describe multiple sclerosis, Alzheimer's disease, myasthenia gravis, Parkinson's disease, and others. Charaka describes many causes of disease including environmental, dietary, and emotional factors. Charaka's concepts are contained in the *Charaka Samhita*, compiled between 100 and 400 B.C.. This is the oldest Ayurvedic text in existence. It discusses anatomy, physiology, pathogenesis, diagnosis, and critically important – prevention. However, it should be noted that the *Charaka Samhita* is most likely a compilation of works of several authors over an extended period, however. The ancient *Charaka Samhita* maintains that the first cause of all illness is the loss of faith in the Divine. While dogs probably do not have any faith in the divine to begin with, the concept that mental and spiritual influences are important in causing and healing illness is critical in Ayurvedic thought.

The *Charaka* lists many practical things one can do in daily life to ward off illness and promote health. It also considered details of disease progression and treatment options such as herbs and oil massages. The *Charaka* presents steps to take in one's daily life to promote health; it also describes causes of disease (such as environmental, dietary, and emotional factors), has many chapters devoted to specific diseases with some details of disease progression, and offers a variety therapeutic measures. It mainly presents herbs, oil massages, and enemas. The heavy reliance on therapeutic massage with specific oils according to the disorder being treated and on enemas (usually made with an oil base) is unique to the Ayurvedic system. However, the use of enemas as a regular therapy is not recommended for animals, who have a somewhat different system.

The second founder, Sushruta, was one of the world's first named surgeons, and accurately described the month by month development of the fetus. His writings are contained in the *Sushruta Samhita,* compiled about the same time as Charaka's work by Nagarjuna, the great Indian philosopher, showing again the intricate connection the Hindus felt between philosophy and science. I often suspect that the severing of these two immensely important fields has been a factor in wars and other conflicts. When science does not have the balancing and restraining hand of philosophy upon its shoulder, scientists see no reason not to create horrific weapons and other tools in the service of violence.

The third founder of Ayurveda, Vaghbata, is the author of two major Ayurvedic works: the *Ashtanga Sangraha* and the *Ashtanga Hridaham.* He was the first person to develop the concept of the sub-doshas, discussed later on. Much of Vagbhatas work is a summary of the writings of the other two writers.

Originally, there were two schools of Ayurvedic medicine, one of surgeons and one of physicians specializing in less invasive techniques. Both schools were recognized as valid, and still are. Today, Ayurveda is divided into eight "specialties": the aforementioned surgery and internal medicine; plus there are additional specialty areas – diseases of the head and neck; toxicology; mental disorders and seizures; pediatrics; geriatrics; theriogenology and sexuality.

However, Ayurvedic medicine does not stand still. Today we have knowledge of many herbal properties (and herbs themselves) unknown to the founders. We know more about physiology and exercise techniques. We may frame some ancient concepts in more up to date language. (A Type A personality, for instance, is really nothing more than, in Ayurvedic terms, a "Vata/Pitta" type person or animal.)

Over a thousand different remedies are listed in these traditional holy texts. Today the best-known proponent of Ayurvedic medicine is Deepak Chopra, M.D., who has written many books on human physical and mental wellness. However, there is no reason to believe that the basic principles of Ayurveda cannot be applied to animals as well.

While mainstream Western medicine is becoming increasingly popular in India, most major cities have an Ayurvedic college and hospital, and, as mentioned before, variations of the system have also been practiced for centuries in Pakistan, Nepal, Bangladesh, Sri Lanka, and Tibet. In the U.S., the professional practice of Ayurveda began to develop in the late 20th century.

Ayurveda and Hindu Philosophy

Ayurveda has deep roots in Hindu philosophies. I use the plural form here, because there are six accepted (orthodox) schools, all of which are based on the Vedas, or Holy Scriptures of Hinduism, the source of all orthodox Indian philosophy. In Indian tradition, these works have no human author, but were "seen" and "sung" into their present form by holy seers called *rishis*.

The word we translate as philosophy, Darshan or Darshana, really means "a way of seeing things." So the Shad Darshanas really means "Six Ways of Seeing." They are Sankhya, Nyaya, Vaisheshika, Mimamsa, Yoga, and Vedanta. Ayurveda makes use of all six philosophies, without trying to "choose between them." Each one contributes something to concepts of healing.

For instance, Nyaya focuses on logic. Yoga, Mimamsa, and Vedanta are more concerned with the eternal, invisible "real world" that underlies the visible, changeful world of appearances. In these practices, philosophers do not regard the physical world as unreal exactly; they simply maintain that there is a deeper reality called Brahman, the Ultimate. Two of the systems, Sankhya and Vaisheshika, deal with the material world as it has evolved from the ultimate.

According to the key Indian view of life, all beings in the universe belong to an ultimate reality which is the source and basis of all. In other words, all entities in the universe participate equally in the Brahman. Physicists have a similar understanding of the world: everything from toads to temples is made up of infinitesimal particles. What is more, these particles are the same for all beings. One electron, for instance, is just like another electron. There are no "toad electrons" or "temple electrons." Electrons are just electrons. There are no "gold electrons" and no "iron electrons", although there are gold atoms and iron atoms. Differences begin to emerge at the elemental and atomic level. A gold atom is different from an iron atom in the number and arrangements of its protons, neutrons, and electrons, but each of these smaller particles is the same for each kind of atom.

In like manner, Ayurvedic medicine takes note of differences among patient types and diseases, while recognizing the fundamental unity that underlies them all. A Kapha type patient will develop a different kind of arthritis than a Vata type patient.

Gregory and Eric may get the same flu virus, but in each person the response is different.

This makes Ayurvedic medicine one of the most flexible, yet stable and coherent of all medical systems. So far, in the West the knowledge of Ayurveda has been shared only among human beings. Yet, India, the home of Ayurvedic practice, is also the birthplace of the first animal hospitals! Every creature, according to Ayurvedic philosophy, has its own *sadhanas,* its special practices or way of living that makes it most at home in the universe. Dogs, for example, have superlative noses and the ability to sense things humans cannot. Humans, on the other hand, have the ability to reason at a high level of abstraction. Yet we share a connection that transcends our differences.

The Question of Karma – and What Is an Animal?

Science recognizes quite clearly that human beings are animals. The same principles of sickness and healing apply to both. The Indian people have always understood the close bonds between domestic animals and their owners, and we all now understand that animals and people can contract many of the same ailments: cancer, heart disease, diabetes, Addison's and Cushing's disease, as well as many of the same psychological and stress-related behavior problems. We are all under attack from bacteria, fungi, and viruses. Antibiotics and vaccinations work the same way in dogs and cats as in people. Both animals and people are capable of being bored, sad, lonely, and irritable. Both can also be happy, calm, and energetic. While western religions have been anxious to look for differences between animals and people, eastern philosophies recognize the deeper kinship between us, a kinship that goes beyond physical similarities, right down to the spirit.

In Hindu philosophy, there is only one soul or spirit that pervades the universe. While all medicinal systems recognize that the body and mind can influence each other, in classical Hindu philosophy, the body and mind are ultimately identical! Modern science is coming around to this point of view as well, but whereas most western scientists believe that the entire organism (mind and body) is ultimately a physical being, the Ayurvedic viewpoint understands that the body and mind are divergent aspects of Brahman.

Your pet will never know he is Brahman, as he is not evolved or aware enough to make the connection (most human beings aren't either). However, whether or not your pet realizes his true state, the fact is that, according to Ayurvedic philosophy, his proper care and training may be undertaken only with this idea in mind. Since your pet is uniquely bound to you, it is up to you to care for his health using the best of your own awareness.

Not only is your pet identical with ultimate reality – you too are identical, in some fundamental way, with your pet. You may be surprised to find how much this understanding changes and improves your relationship with your dog!

However, until we are fully enlightened, that fact is difficult to comprehend. After all, even if the world really *is* single, uniform and changeless, it *seems* to be manifold, variable, and in flux. This is called Maya, the ordinary, lived experience of the Cosmos. In physics, we may understand that a table is *really* mostly empty space, but we have no qualms about putting a heavy turkey platter on top of it. Thus in our ordinary life we are forced to deal with spiritual reality as we understand it at the moment, not as it really is. That true view of reality is saved for moments of insight or deep meditation.

Ordinary reality undergoes many fluctuations and transmutations, at least in appearance. Although in deepest reality we are all one, the true understanding of that fact, which is called liberation, is a long and difficult process. Ayurveda is alone among medical therapies in that it takes into account both our universal, changeless, eternal nature and the unique complex of physical and mental attributes that makes each being upon earth one-of-a-kind. According to Ayurveda, each of us is a microcosm of the eternally changing, yet ultimate changeless universe. We are all different – and all the same. The individual spirit may live many lifetimes before it finds that freedom which is its true birthright. Some of those lives may be spent in the animal world.

In Hinduism and its daughter Buddhism, animals belong to an order of beings who are less enlightened than humans, although we are all brothers under the skin (or fur). Because of this animals suffer more, and it is our job, as humans, to ease those sufferings and help them along the path towards fuller realization. Who knows? The family cat may return as your brother-in-law!

The concept that we live many lives, and that each life is the result of the ones before is called karma. The word literally means *action* and it simply means that one's actions, physical, mental, or spiritual, have consequences, not just in this life, but over many lifetimes. Karma is another way of talking about cause and effect. While it is readily understood that physical actions have physical consequences (drinking too much gives people a hangover), it took western science quite a while to realize what ordinary people and Ayurveda have always known: that losing a loved is truly a heart-ache, that guilt makes you sick, and spiritual happiness can make physical pain disappear or at least seem unimportant.

In Ayurveda for humans, clients are urged to become responsible for their own health. Since domestic animals have little choice but to depend upon their caretakers for a healthy lifestyle, we realize what a tremendous responsibility this is. You are responsible for your pet's health.

Domestic animals occupy a special place in the scheme of things. They are not wild but they aren't human either. Because we humans have in a sense "created" them, we have a special duty and responsibility towards them. We also have a special connection, a unique bond. That is why Ayurveda is a team effort. While it does rely on physical methods such as herbs and exercise to promote health, it also makes use of spiritual resources. Here is where you can be beneficial to your pet as well as to yourself. Ayurveda is more than a system of medicine – it's a whole lifestyle for both of you!

Ayurvedic medicine offers a plethora of treatment options, which actually work side by side with and enhance mainstream western veterinary care. As mentioned earlier, this is a truly holistic modality that draws upon many sources, including diet, exercise, crystals, aromas, sound, and psychological therapy. It "keeps up" with the times while remaining true to its original principles. It strongly focuses on disease prevention and the need to live in harmony with nature, of which we are all a part. More than any other system of medicine, Ayurveda focuses on preventive care and the lifestyle changes that make disease less likely to occur in the first place. For both humans and pets, this means proper exercise, rest, diet, emotional support, and attitude.

It's All in the Balance

Balance and equilibrium are key words in Ayurvedic practice. A healthy state is a balanced state. But balance is not always easy to achieve. Animals and humans are constantly bombarded with bacteria, viruses, weather changes, new life situations, accidents, diet changes, and more. Every one of these things can affect the equilibrium in the body, mind, and spirit. When these three are in perfect balance, the self is in a state of health.

It is the goal of Ayurvedic medicine to help make the necessary responses to these changes and to do the basic things that make the patient more fully able to respond himself, without unnecessary outside intervention. It should be noted that death is the common fate of all creatures. It is a necessary transition to a new state of being. Therefore, health in this life is always somewhat precarious, can never be absolutely assured, and in the long run will fail. Death is a part of the cycle that cannot be waved away. However, it is possible to look for ways to achieve a healthy lifespan for our pets and ourselves. Simply because all physical systems ultimately fail is no reason not to keep them in good working order as long as is reasonable. Mental systems also break down. The soul, however, does not fail – it is the part that progresses to a new life. The body and mind are in its service in this life – to prepare it for the next.

Body, mind, and soul operate on a complex and dynamic balance between three forms of energy or Dosha (*Vata, Pitta,* and *Kapha*) and three fundamental aspects of the individual: body, mind, and spirit. These elements interpenetrate and interact with each other. When the fundamental energies and elements of the person are not in balance, there is sickness, depression, slowness of thought, and a spiritual burden. When in balance, the person (whether human-person or animal-person) is healthy, focused, energetic, and free from spiritual burden.

In Ayurveda, illness is as much a thought process as a physical state. Understanding the True Self means gaining right understanding of the body as a part of the entire mental, physical, and spiritual cosmos.

Life is Purposeful

While most animals have enough to do being animals, humans are in a different situation. We are purpose seekers, and for most of us, living a life without meaning is a worthless endeavor. In Hindu philosophy, the ultimate goal of all life is liberation: liberation from ignorance, selfishness, cruelty, and pain. Liberation is finally achievable only after many, many lives, some of them animal, some of them human. It is attainable only after vast experience and suffering. Because we understand that suffering is so deeply ingrained in life, it is one major duty of humans to try to alleviate it. Our pets depend upon us. Now domesticated, they have lost the wild freedom they once enjoyed as they share our lives and have become part of our families. It was a risky bargain – and now we owe it to them to do our part. As Charaka wrote, "A physician, though well versed in the knowledge and treatment of disease, who does not enter into the heart of the patient with the virtue of light and love, will not be able to heal the patient." This is why you as the owner of your pet have the best chance to heal him. You are the one who loves him. And love is the best medicine of all.

Cosmic Energy

Everything begins with energy, for energy was born with the universe. It did not have to evolve out of it, the way palm trees and sewer rats and wolves did. Many people know that the working basis of Ayurvedic medicine is the division of creatures into three basic types: Vata, Pitta, and Kapha. What is less understood is where these types come from, and what they mean in the scheme of things. They did not spring out of nowhere!

In Ayurvedic theory, every creature in the universe was created either by "male" energy, *Purusha,* or "female" energy, *Prakriti.* (This word is sometimes transliterated *Prakruti,* with people from northern India using the "i" sound, and people from southern India the "u" sound. Both are equally correct. When this word is transliterated from Sanskrit, it is most properly written *Prakṛti,* with a dot below the "r," signaling a hard "r" sound.) In any case, and however you pronounce it, this energy concept comes directly from Sankhya philosophy. The terms "male" and "female" are largely symbolic in this context and do not refer to gender. Both kinds of energy are eternal, and both are present in all the entities of the universe – male and female, animal and human, plant and object. (Much of Ayurvedic metaphysics draws its principles from the philosophy of Sankhya.)

Purusha and *Prakriti* are complementary energies that work together, not opposite forces that fight. In Ayurvedic theory, the universe is born from the powerful and necessary attraction that exists between these two primal energies.

Purusha and Prakriti: The Twin Forces

Everyone has sensed the pulsing of two complementary forces in the universe: male and female, night and day, active and passive, and so on. The concept of *Purusha* and *Prakriti* were developed in Sankhya school of philosophy to account for this universally acknowledged phenomenon. It provides a theoretical underpinning for many Ayurvedic concepts.

In Hindu and Tantric philosophy in general, it is the female force that is regarded as the active, creative force, while in western traditional philosophy, the male force plays that role. The distinction is not important; it is the idea of the complementary forces that counts.

In Ayurvedic theory, the "male" force, *Purusha,* is passive, pure, formless awareness or pure consciousness. It acts more as witness than as a working force. In an important sense, it is outside time and space.

Prakriti is active, day-to-day consciousness and will. It is vibrant, colorful, and creative. It makes choices. It is said that from the womb of Prakriti the whole universe is born. The Prakriti remains fairly constant throughout one's life, although it is, of course, subject to outside influences. It is also said that Prakriti depends upon Purusha for its existence, although the reverse is not true. The relationship between Purusha and Prakriti develops and becomes more complex, and they "give birth" to a procession of manifestations.

The first manifestation of Prakriti is *Mahad* or *Mahat,* the great universal order or creative, undifferentiated intelligence. In the Ayurvedic tradition, this faculty is present in every living cell. For example, each cell knows how to use the nutrients provided to it without having to study it in a book. This primordial knowledge is sometimes called cellular intelligence and is, as I said, possessed by every living thing.

The second, more individualized, everyday manifestation of Prakriti is *Ahamkara,* the separate, individual ego or self-identity, although it means much more than that. (You may be able to see the roots of "I am" in this ancient Sanskrit word.) It comes directly from Mahad, the more general intelligence, just as the knowledge that eight plus eight equal sixteen is based on general principles. Ahamkara is the part of the self that carries over from life to life and does not perish with the body. It bears within itself all its previous births and experiences.

This self is created from its genetic heritage, its karmic past, and its present experiences in this life; it does not reference just human beings, but all creation. The Ahamkara is a centered, bounded self. This is the personal ego. When you stand and look around you, it appears as if you are the center the universe. In a larger sense we understand this is not so, but it appears to each of us to be true. This is even more applicable to dogs, who cannot be expected to understand about Mahad. (It's even beyond the reach of some human beings.) The world of the dog is bounded by Ahamkara. For people, the ultimate realization of Ahamkara, is Buddhi, the Wakened Intellect, the part of the individual self who knows he is also the Mahad or universal self. In a word, it is Enlightenment.

The Gunas or Main Qualities of Existence

However, every self is different. The quality or kind of individual self, what differentiates one being from another, is largely determined by the Gunas (universal qualities), which is how the self is "broken up." Hindu philosophy recognizes three fundamental Gunas.

- *Sattva:* Clarity of perception, purity, stability, light, potential energy, creation (pure space on a cosmic level). It is sometimes represented by the Elephant, and may be compared to the subjective world.
- *Tamas:* Confusion, deep sleep, inertia, darkness, destruction (the earth). It is sometimes represented by the Jackal, and may be compared to the objective world.

- *Rajas:* Movement, change, dynamism, and kinetic energy, preservation (the atmosphere). It is sometimes represented by the Tiger, and represents the energy that flows between the other two Gunas.

The Gunas are the energies of the mind, and as in people, they are present in varying degrees among different types of dogs. All individuals, of course, have all three gunas, just as they have all three Doshas (next chapter). Doshas are continuously being formed and re-formed by food, physical and mental activity, and by the bodily processes. But while the Doshas are primarily qualities of the body and feelings, the Gunas are more basic; they are qualities of the mind or spirit. The Gunas are "real," but they are not independent. Each Guna depends on the others, and everything in the universe is a result of their various combinations. Altogether, they make up the *Mansa Prakriti,* or dominant characteristic of each individual.

Sattva equips an individual with the ability to have clarity of perception. It is responsible for the creation of mind, as well as the five sense faculties (ears, skin, eyes, nose, tongue), and the five "motor organs" or organs of action: mouth, hands, feet, genitals, and excretory organs. Sattva is the "knower" or the "observer."

Tamas is responsible for periods of confusion and deep sleep, as well as the tendency towards inertia and darkness. It is responsible for the creation of matter and the five elements: space, air, fire, water, and earth and the sensation that belong to each: sound and space, touch and air, sight and fire, taste and water, smell and earth. Tamas is the object of knowledge" or "the object of observation."

Rajas cause dynamic movement, sensations, feelings and emotions, everything that makes us animals. It is the "process of observation." It is the active force that mediates between Sattva and Tamas.

This ancient view of the world and senses is somewhat at variance with the contemporary scientific view, but the two ways of organizing the cosmos are not contradictory. The contemporary view is based on scientifically determined "fact." The classical Hindu view is a more metaphoric, poetic approach that is nonetheless "true" in that it has a philosophic coherence and gets results.

It may seem strange to think of all the elements in the world as a mixture of only three basic substances; however, this threefold division of the universe is seen everywhere, from science to folklore: animal, vegetable, mineral. Gas, liquid, solid; proton, electron, neutron; fats, protein, carbohydrates; mind, body, soul. We will see in the next chapter that Ayurvedic medicine also divides beings into three types (Doshas): Vata, Pitta, and Kapha. The concept of sattva/tamas/rajas is both natural and logical.

The Five Elements of the Cosmos

In Ayurvedic thought, the Gunas combine in various ways to form the five fundamental elements *(panchmahabhuta)* of the physical universe and of sensory perception.

Each element is significant in itself, but also represents a state of Brahman or the Ultimate, and each is an important symbol of life. Each element is also connected metaphorically to a particular body organ or function and is as mentioned composed of one or more of the three Gunas.

- Earth *(Prithvi)* is composed of Tamas
- Water *(Jal)* is composed of Tamas and Sattva
- Fire *(Agni)* is composed of intense Rajas and Sattva
- Air *(Vayu)* is composed of Sattva and Rajas
- Ether or Space *(Akasha)* is composed of Sattva

Each element reflects the quality of the Gunas that made it. The earth, for example, is heavy, thick, dark, and uncomprehending, like Tamas, the unconscious force.

At the other end of the spectrum, ether is empty, clear, containing pure Sattva. Air is clear also, but moves swiftly, and so contains Rajas. Water is also clear, but heavy and so contains Tamas. Fire is mostly energy (in its most intense form), but has a brilliant clarity about it, and so contains Rajas. Thus all the elements but earth contain at least some Sattva.

In the Ayurvedic understanding of life, these five elements exist not just in the world outside the body, but in every part of the body as well. Each body, in fact is made of the five elements, which often work in pairs to accomplish their work. Thus, ***Earth*** *(prithvi)* represents matter in its solid state. It signifies strength, rigidity, and also structural body parts such as bones, teeth, and cell walls. It is considered heavy, dull, dense, static, hard, and coarse. It is the physical body, and is related to the nose and sense of smell (although it has strong connections to all physical senses), as well as to memory. Scientists are just now learning the deep connection between smell and memory. Smell is the only sense that can linger after its maker is gone. In the dog world, when another dog passes by, its smell remains long after its sight and sound or physical presence has gone. Bloodhounds have been known to track a scent that is 100 hours old! We humans have an attenuated sense of smell and can only marvel at this almost magical ability, which connects the dog firmly to the earth. Some contemporary practitioners associate it with physical energy.

Water *(jal)* represents fluidity and change. Water is defined in Ayurvedic literature as cool, liquid, dull, soft, oily, and slimy. (This isn't a very attractive picture of water, but it can indeed carry all those qualities.) Most of your pet's body is made from water, and changes constantly. The blood, saliva, urine, and lymph are the primary body parts represented by water. Water is related to the tongue and the sense of taste. Some contemporary practitioners associate it with chemical energy (water is the nearly universal solvent, after all).

Fire *(agni)* is the transforming element. It is considered hot, sharp, light, dry, and subtle. In the body it works along with digestion/metabolism, the nervous system, and mental processes. It is represented by the body's acids and enzymes and is carried through the body in the blood and plasma as heat. In more metaphoric terms, Agni persists as the hidden witness of our every birth and rebirth. In traditional thought, there are thirteen different kinds of Agni!

In Ayurvedic medicine, Agni is most closely related to vision and the eye, and most of us have indeed seen the "fire" in a pet's eye! Fire is also connected to intelligence, as we can see when we use the words "bright" and "brilliant" to refer to mental abilities. "I see" is another way of saying "I understand" and an illuminating talk or book gives "insight," another visual word. The ancient Rishis or singers of the Vedas, were "seers" who saw into the heart of things, and "Ayurveda" is connected with the word for vision, sight, and knowledge (which share the same root). Some contemporary practitioners associate it with radiant energy. (A related use of the term Agni, refers to the "digestive fire," which we will talk about later.)

Air *(vayu)* represents respiration and breath. It is dry, light, rough, cold, subtle, and mobile; in fact it is the very principle of movement. In traditional thought, it is most closely related to the sense of touch and to the skin. All sensory responses are considered to be due to the subtle motions of Prana, the breath of life. In the body it is the element that powers the movements of blood and food and lymph through the body. In the form of breath (Prana) it is life itself, and Prana is the foundational principle of the air element. Some contemporary practitioners associate it with electrical energy.

Ether *(akasha)* is the space or environment in which the body and mind live. It is the subtlest of the five elements and is said to be clear, light, subtle, soft, and immeasurable. The word *Akasha* has an almost mystical significance in the Hindu tradition. *Akasha* is moveless, all-pervading, and universal. It is freedom. It is emptiness. It is the home for all other aspects of existence, and comes before all the others. It is the universal super-consciousness. In traditional thought, it is most closely related to the organ of hearing. The hearing of sacred mantras in Ayurvedic medicine resonates throughout this subtle element. Some contemporary practitioners associate it with nuclear energy.

All these elements are present in every being, and in every part of every being. Take a single living cell. Each cell occupies a space *(Akasha)*. The structural walls of the cells are denoted by the Earth element *(Prithvi)*, the cytoplasm within the cell is the water *(Jal)*, the cell's metabolic processes are fire, and the gases within it are air. In a more complex system such as the whole body, the bones and teeth are dominated by the earth element *(Prithvi)*, digestion and metabolism by fire *(Agni)*, the bodily fluids by water *(Jal)*, and the being's mobility and movement by air *(Vayu)*. Again, all takes place within the Akasha.

Together, they form the *prakriti*, our normal consciousness. Each element also has its own physical sense associated with it: Ether is traditionally associated with *shabda* (sound); air with *sparsha* (touch); fire with *rupa* (form or sight); water with *rasa* (taste) and earth with *gandha* (smell).

Finally, the five elements combine together in various ways to form the three major body/personality types: Vatta, Pitta, or Kapha. "Typing" your dog into one of these types is a major step in Ayurvedic healing. We will look at this in detail in the following chapter.

In Ayurveda, the key to a healthy life is *swastha* – balance. Balance between gunas, between elements, between ways of perception. For dogs, as for humans, too much or too little food, too much loneliness (or even surprisingly, too much attention), overwork or too little exercise, all can destroy the delicate balance, the endless dance between body, mind, and soul that keeps us whole.

Chapter 2

The Doshas: Typing Your Pet

One of the most important concepts in Ayurveda is that of the *Doshas*, the three major influences upon every living being. There are three doshas (Tridoshas): Vata, Pitta, and Kapha. Each of these "bodily humors" is composed from two of the five classical elements: space, air, fire, water, and earth.

The five elements combine in dynamic pairs to powerfully affect our health. This action is called dosha, and each dosha has a predominant element. Vata is air and ether; Pitta is water and fire; Kapha is composed of water and earth. The proportion of the two elements in each dosha determines how active the dosha is. Every physical, mental, emotional, and spiritual characteristic of every being is influenced (and can be explained by) the action of the Tridoshas. While we may refer to a being as a "Vata" individual, we only mean that that person (or dog) has a lot of the Vata dosha operating within him.

The concept of *doshas* goes all the way back to the ancient sage Charaka, who wrote about them in the fifth century B.C., *Charaka Samhita*. The word "dosha" literally means "fault," since none of the doshas alone comprises the entire self. In addition, the dosha is a sort of waste product that moves out of the body even as it performs its vital functions. The dosha known as Vata, for example, expresses itself partly in the breath – but breathing in requires breathing out. If a dosha over-accumulates in the body, it can cause disease as much as if the dosha were missing or lacking.

For perfect health in all spheres, the doshas must be balanced – that doesn't mean they must be equal in every individual, but be balanced in such a way that is natural for that being. Vata dogs naturally produce more Vata than Kapha or Pitta dogs. Because Vata dogs are so strongly naturally Vata, adding a lot of Vata-producing foods to his diet might over-balance him in the Vata direction and lead to illness. As we shall see in the following chapters, the wise body tells us not only when it is losing its natural balance, but also in what direction it is losing that balance, by characteristic signs that we call "symptoms."

The stage in which a dosha builds up is called the "accumulation" phase. When it reaches the stage that causes disease or imbalance, it is called "provocation" or "aggravation." The stage in which a dosha begins to subside, either naturally or with the help of diet and environmental therapy, is called "pacification." It is quite natural for the dosha to flow through the body in a cycle like this. We are not static beings!

Doshas not only build up in the body but also inhabit certain seasons of the year. Pitta, for example, starts to accumulate in the late spring and reaches its height (provocation) in summer. Vata begins in the early fall and reaches its height in early winter. And Kapha starts to accumulate in winter, reaching its height in spring.

However, dosha is not a simple concept to grasp – nor does the understanding what your pet's dosha is lead miraculously to perfect health. Many other factors influence health. The dosha is only a place to start.

The terms Vata, Pitta, and Kapha bear a resemblance to the western scientific designation of body types Ectomorph, Mesomorph, and Endomorph, although the Ayurvedic understanding is more comprehensive and includes more than just body type.

No single individual dog is a pure dosha-type, but it is usually not hard to tell which dosha predominates.

In like manner, dog breeds as well as individual dogs have predilections. For example, Vata tends to predominate in most Salukis; Pitta in Boxers; and Kapha in Bulldogs, but there is plenty of individual variation.

A Vata Bulldog is probably not as Vata as even a Kapha Saluki, but is more Vata than most of his breed. Most individuals have more than one dosha. For example, a Vata-Kapha dog might be tall like a Vata type, but have a heavier build and resemble Kapha in other aspects. This sort of dog has more insulation against cold than a pure Kapha type, and is often used for cold-weather jobs like sled-racing.

Most animals (including the human animal) have one predominant dosha, with a secondary dosha contribution. Few individuals are almost purely one dosha, and even fewer are "balanced" between the three doshas. I suspect many highly placed conformation or show dogs fall into the "tridosha" category. A tri-balanced individual sounds ideal, but it can be a precarious state of affairs. A tri-doshic can become ill when there is an imbalance that might be "natural" for a Vata or Pitta or Kapha individual. Such finely tuned dogs need extra help to keep those three competing doshas in balance.

Individuals with only one type (Vata, Pitta, or Kapha) are considered monotypes. Of the dual types, the most common, are Vata-Pitta (or Pitta-Vata), Pitta-Kapha (or Kapha-Pitta), and Kapha-Vata (or Vata-Kapha). While Pitta-Kapha and Kapha-Pitta types both combine Pitta and Kapha, the dosha listed first is predominant. The balanced or triple type is, of course, Vata-Pitta-Kapha.

The general goal in Ayurvedic therapy is for each individual to achieve his natural balance, that is, a balance natural to his own personal dosha and the circumstances of his life. Ayurveda understands that each being is unique. Balancing the doshas does not automatically mean an equal amount of Vata, Pitta, and Kapha. It means balancing the doshas with which the animal was born. You can't turn a typical Pitta-type dog into a Vata- or Kapha-type, and you probably don't want to. It means to maintain the "natural balance" for that individual. All doshas are present to at least some extent in every individual.

It is believed that the particular combination of Vata-Pitta-Kapha contained in the egg and sperm at time of fertilization combine in new ways to partly determine the energy constellation, the *Prakriti,* or structure of the new being. It should be very clear that all three dosha exist throughout the whole body in every cell; however, their balance is different depending upon where they are.

Disease may originate within the body from hereditary or dosha-related factors; it may come from outside the body, as in trauma, bacteria, or viruses, or may even have a supernatural cause such as a curse or planetary influence.

It should be noted that a particular disease might be caused by more than one dosha disorder. Both Vata and Pitta disorders might manifest themselves in intestinal problems, but the presentation of the problem will be different due to the different causes. As in mainstream medicine, Ayurveda is complex – just like the body.

In their normal measure, the doshas act as supporters for the bodily functions. Only when they appear to be in imbalance or excess should they be called pathological or "faults," (even though that is what the word technically means).

It should always be remembered that the Tridosha is an extremely complex and elaborate theory, with many variations on the doshas, and many, many influences coming to bear on them. Although body type and diet are critical factors, they are certainly not the only ones.

In Ayurvedic theory there are 20 qualities that can influence the increase or decrease of the doshas. Often these qualities are found in food, but they are often inherent in other substances such as events, weather, and relationships. For example, light, dry sharp winds increase Vata, while heavy, sticky weather and fog increase Kapha. These 20 qualities are:

- ***Guru*** (Heavy): Increases Kapha and decreases Vata and Pitta.
- ***Laghu*** (Light): Increases Vata and Pitta and decreases Kapha.
- ***Manda*** (Slow or Dull): Increases Kapha and decreases Vata and Pitta.
- ***Tikshna*** (Sharp): Increases Vata and Pitta and decreases Kapha.
- ***Shita*** (Cold): Increases Vata and Kapha and decreases Pitta.
- ***Ushna*** (Hot): Increases Pitta and decreases Vata and Kapha.
- ***Snigdha*** (Oily): Increases Pitta and decreases Vata and Kapha.
- ***Ruksha*** (Dry): Increases Vata and decreases Pitta and Kapha.
- ***Shlakshna*** (Smooth, slimy): Increases Pitta and Kapha and decreases Vata.
- ***Khara*** (Rough): Increases Vata and decreases Pitta and Kapha.
- ***Sandra*** (Dense): Increases Kapha and decreases Vata and Pitta.
- ***Drava*** (Liquid): Increases Pitta and Kapha and decreases Vata.
- ***Mrudu*** (Soft): Increases Pitta and Kapha and decreases Vata.
- ***Kathina*** (Hard): Increases Vata and Kapha and decreases Pitta.
- ***Sthira*** (Static): Increases Kapha and decreases Vata and Pitta.
- ***Chala*** (Mobile): Increases Vata and Pitta and decreases Kapha.
- ***Sukshma*** (Subtle): Increases Vata and Pitta and decreases Kapha.
- ***Sthula*** (Gross): Increases Kapha and decreases Vata and Pitta.

- ***Vishada*** (Clear): Increases Vata and Pitta and decreases Kapha.
- ***Picchila*** (Sticky): Increases Kapha and decreases Vata and Pitta.

Doshas often share one quality with another dosha. The third dosha does not contain this quality, and in this instance can be considered its "opposite." For example, Vata and Pitta are both "light," while Kapha is "heavy." Vata and Kapha are both "cold," while Pitta is "hot." Pitta and Kapha are both "oily," while Vata is "dry." In the realm of food, cold foods tend to increase Kapha and Vata, but decrease Pitta. Heavy foods increase Kapha but decrease Vata and Pitta. Oily foods decrease Vata and increase Pitta and Kapha. And so on.

Some authorities list the twentieth quality as Avila *(Cloudy) rather than* Piccila *(Sticky). It has approximately the same effect.*

If you plan on having more than one dog, it generally works out that like types get along better than different or contrasting types.

Vata

Air and ether combine to form the dosha known as *Vata,* which means "wind," or more scientifically, perhaps, "anabolism," the process that builds up material. Vata is the major body principle, and its main element is air. We shouldn't confuse this kind of "air," however, with the air that circulates through the atmosphere. This air is "subtle energy," Vata is the dosha of energy (*Rajas*). Most Vata dogs have a lot of *rajas* in them! Vata is often considered the most dominant of all the doshas. It controls breathing, movement, the nervous system, heartbeat, eye blinks, cell movements, and emotions such as lightness, "ungroundedness," fear, and anxiety. Vata is so important because, as it moves, it is commonly said to maintain the balance between the other two doshas, Pitta and Kapha, which are more inert.

Vata is stored in the colon and adjacent parts and "rules" the lower body. Disorders in the Vata probably cause more diseases than in the other two doshas combined; thus it is of central importance.

Vata, like each of the other doshas, has five subparts, called Airs. These are:

- ***Prana*** is located in the brain, heart, chest, and face. Prana gives the power of life to the body, the so-called "cosmic breath," and is connected to the sympathetic nervous system, part of the nervous system that accelerates the heart rate, constricts blood vessels, and raises blood pressure. Prana is the author of all sensations. It is the controller of breath, sneezing, belching, digestion, circulation, and the mind, in fact, all "outward movement." When disturbed or out of balance, it can lead to throat and lung problems.
- ***Udana*** moves upward from the umbilicus through the lungs to the throat and nose. The word "udana" means "upward moving." It centers in the throat and is connected to the parasympathetic nervous system (the part of the nervous system that originates in the brain stem and lower spinal cord that in many ways works in opposition to the sympathetic nervous system, slowing the heart rate, and so on) and also has to do with speech. Ayurveda practitioners often refer to it as the "clock," referring to the number of breaths each being is granted. When udana is strong, the dog is intelligent, trainable (and often vocal). Weakened udana results in loss of cognitive ability, particularly as we see in canine cognitive dysfunction. When disturbed or out of balance, it can lead to diseases of the eye, ear nose and throat.
- ***Samana*** flows through the digestive tract, is the air of "balance" and helps preserve the equilibrium between the mind and the spirit. It is located near the digestive fire (*Agni*). It mostly resides in the middle area of the body and holds food in the alimentary tract. When disturbed or out of balance, it can lead to food assimilation difficulties and digestive problems.
- ***Apana*** centers in the colon and pelvic region, controls the expulsion of urine and feces. It also controls the genitals and keeps the fetus in good health. The word "apana" means "downward moving." When disturbed or out of balance, it can lead to diseases of the anal glands, rectum, urinary tract, and even diabetes.

- ***Vyana*** is diffused through the body, but centers in the heart and moves through the body with the circulation. A being well stocked with vyana is accommodating and gentle. When disturbed or out of balance, it can lead to circulatory diseases.

Vata Dogs

- Have plenty of restless energy
- Are quick-thinking
- Thrive on a regular routine
- Are light sleepers and good watchdogs
- Are generally friendly with other dogs and people
- Have strong need for both emotional and physical warmth
- Dislike winter and cold weather
- Have a tendency towards thinness
- May appear physically underdeveloped
- May have curly or kinky hair coat
- May have a poor coat and dry skin and do well on omega-3 supplements.
- May have brittle or overly tough nails (and hate having them cut)
- Are long-lived; however many seem to suffer more illnesses
- May be unpredictable and easily agitated
- Tends towards psychological disorders such as fear, nervous problems, noise phobias, anxiety
- Tend towards physical problems such as bloat, flatulence, constipation, and other digestive trouble, arthritis (especially in the back) and other bone or joint problems, poor bite, spasms
- May bark excessively.

The well-balanced Vata dog is a happy and adaptable. (They make superior therapy dogs.) Vata dogs enjoy quiet times with their owners, and benefit from just "hanging out." When Vata builds up, it creates the following adverse emotional problems: anxiety, fear, nervousness, giddiness, insecurity, phobias, restlessness, and confusion.

The Vata dog is about 75 percent *rajas,* 20 percent *sattva,* and only 5 percent *tamas*. Vata (in all dosha types) tends to increase with age. It also increases in areas with dry climates and during cold, windy falls and early winter. These dogs do best if kept warm and calm. The best colors for Vata dogs' collars, beds, and sweaters are earth tones, red, green, and orange, or combinations thereof.

Diseases of the Vata type include bladder, colon, anal and heart problems, tremors, arthritis, and low vitality. In many ways Vata dogs are the most complex of the main types. Most belong to "primitive" breed types and seem less domestic and less evolved than Pitta or Kapha types. Vata dogs are truly different and people who have owned only Pitta and Kapha type dogs before are in for a surprise. These are dogs that follow their own nature. The symbolic animal for the Vata dog is the antelope and if you think of your Vata dog as a swift footed, elegant, but essentially wild antelope or gazelle you will be well on your way to understanding your pet's true character.

Mature human beings of the Kapha-Pitta, Pitta-Kapha, or Kapha-Vata types make the best owners of Vata dogs.

Although every individual dog is different, the following breeds have a high percentage of Vata dogs: Afghan Hound, Borzoi, Dalmatian, Greyhound, Ibizan Hound, Irish Setter, Irish Wolfhound, Pharaoh Hound, Saluki, and Whippet.

Pitta

Fire and water combine to form the Dosha known as *Pitta,* or metabolism. The word Pitta comes ultimately from the Sanskrit word "tapas," which means to heat up. Metabolism is the process that converts matter (food) into energy, such as movement and thought. Pitta controls the enzymatic and hormonal activity, the digestive processes, metabolism, hunger and thirst, body temperature, skin type and pigmentation, the luster of the eyes, intelligence, and understanding. Interestingly, in Ayurvedic thought, digestion is the most important function of the body, and poor digestion is the source of most disease. Pitta controls the central part of the body. Like fire, Pitta is the force of transformation.

Emotionally, too much Pitta arouses anger, hatred, and jealousy. It is stored in the small intestine, bile, stomach, sweat glands, blood, fat, eyes, and skin. Too little Pitta results in indigestion, sluggish metabolism, and dullness of mind. Too much can produce ulcers, hormonal imbalance, irritated skin, and anger. It is most common in hot summers and in adolescent and adult pets.

The five Pitta sub-doshas are called "Fires. They are:

- ***Alochaka,*** located in the pupil and retina of the eyes, governs vision. When disturbed or out of balance, it can lead to impairment of vision.
- ***Bhrajaka,*** diffused throughout the body, governs skin. When disturbed or out of balance, it can lead to skin disease.
- ***Sadhaka,*** based in the heart, governs desire, mental function, drive, and feelings. It governs memory retention. When disturbed or out of balance, it can lead to cardiac and psychological problems.
- ***Pachaka,*** located in the stomach and small intestine, governs digestion and absorption of food. It exists as non-liquid heat, bile, or digestive fire. When disturbed or out of balance, it can lead to indigestion.
- ***Ranjaka,*** located in the liver, spleen, and stomach, governs the liver, and secondarily the stomach and spleen. It controls blood formation. When disturbed or out of balance, it can lead to anemia, and various kinds of liver problems.

Pitta Dogs

- Have a strong, moderate build – these are usually extremely handsome dogs
- May have pointed noses
- Tend to be less hairy than Vata dogs
- Are intelligent
- Are impatient and short tempered
- Are good with cats
- Have a tendency toward dominance and, if challenged, may not yield
- Make excellent drug-sniffing or other working dogs
- Are hardworking, focused, and energetic
- Have a good appetite and digestion
- Need smaller, more frequent meals
- Dislike hot weather and bright light
- Tend to be more nocturnal than other dogs
- Tend towards the following physical problems: indigestion, diarrhea, cataracts, glaucoma, stomach/ digestive disorders, Cushing's disease, Addison's disease, diabetes, hives, fever, rashes, and other skin problems
- Have loud barks

- Have a tendency towards jealousy, irritability, anger, impatience, and aggression.

The Pitta dog is about 50 percent *sattva,* 45 percent *rajas,* and only about 5 percent *tamas.*

The balanced Pitta dog is athletic, stable, strong, and focused. It is a good endurance pet, and most are highly intelligent and quick-witted. Some are not very patient, however. Pitta dogs benefit from lots of positive playtime and love.

Pitta dogs need to be kept cool in the summer for their physical and emotional health. Summer poses the greatest health challenges. Pitta dogs are more independent than other dogs and require less emotional coddling. This is a dog that can lose control very fast, and can be dangerous when it does.

The best sweater and collar colors for a Pitta dog are white, blue, lavender, purple, mauve, green, and pastels.

Pittas can be thought of as dragon dogs, and that is their symbolic animal. Handling a Pitta dog as if he were a powerful and magical dragon will bring the best results. The best owners of Pitta type dogs are Kapha, Kapha-Pitta, and Pitta-Kapha types. Vata-type owners are generally too weak-willed to control them.

The following breeds have a high percentage of Pitta: Terriers, protective breeds, and working or herding dogs.

Kapha

Water and earth combine to form the dosha known as *Kapha.* Its main element is water. Kapha provides structure and lubrication for the body, or in some renderings of the theory, catabolism, the process that breaks down material. It controls the immune system, wound repair, joint lubrications, mucous secretions, memory retention, and the emotions of clinginess, greed, and long-standing envy. It occupies the intercellular spaces of the body. In correct balance, it supplies calmness and forgiveness. It is stored in the chest. Too little Kapha can result in a dry respiratory tract, stomach problems, and an inability to concentrate. Kapha rules the upper part of the body and also regulates Pitta and Vata.

The Kapha pet is easy-going, laid-back, and relaxed. Of all the dosha types, Kaphas probably most appreciate being talked to, even if they don't understand what you are saying. Kapha dogs may tend to obesity, and they move with slow deliberation. They have soft, often greasy skin. This is a gentle-tempered pet that is slow to anger. Flaws in his temperament include over-attachment, possessiveness, and greed. When the Kapha dog does have a temperament problem, it is usually related to possessiveness. The Kapha dog is about 75 percent *tamas,* 20 percent *sattva,* and only about 5 percent *rajas.*

The five Kapha sub-doshas are called "Waters":

- ***Tarpaka*** governs the lubrication of the eyes, mouth, nose, and the brain and spinal column. It flows in the head and controls emotional well-being. When disturbed or out of balance, it can lead to memory problems.
- ***Bodhaka*** governs taste and the tongue. When disturbed, it can lead to digestive problems.
- ***Kledaka*** originates in the stomach and governs the digestive juices and orders the thinking process. It liquefies hard food masses (very important for dogs who swallow bones and rawhides). When disturbed or out of balance, it can lead to digestive problems.
- ***Avalambaka,*** which flows in the heart, governs plasma and is the ultimate water-source for the other sub-doshas. It is also said to make the limbs flexible and strong. When disturbed or out of balance, it can lead to laziness.
- ***Sleshaka,*** located in the joints, is responsible for joint lubrication. It is said to form a sort of "protective gel." When disturbed or out of balance, it can lead to joint pain.

Kapha Dogs

- Are solid, heavily built
- Are methodical, calm
- Have large beautiful eyes
- Have strong, shiny nails
- Have thick, heavy coat
- Tend towards short noses
- Sleep a lot
- Are well-behaved and trainable as puppies
- Have excellent long-term memories
- Are very attached to and dependent on their owners and suffer if the relationship between the owner and dog is not healthy

- Have difficulty accepting change
- Tend toward ailments such as respiratory problems, allergies, and joint pain
- Are possessive and gluttonous
- Have a strong liking for sweets
- Are couch potatoes
- Are good with birds and large dogs

The balanced Kapha dog is loyal and strong. When Kapha builds up, it tends to create the following emotional problems: gluttony, over-attachment, possessiveness (especially food-possessiveness), boredom, lethargy, and obsessive-compulsive behavior.

In general Kapha dogs are probably the healthiest of all types, but problems with digestion, certain respiratory conditions, and water in the joints can occur. Like Vata, Kapha is considered a "cold" Dosha and Kapha dogs require emotional warmth. These dogs have the most health problems in the later winter and early spring, as well as during a full moon. Kapha dogs need exercise and a light diet to keep them in trim. These dogs are in serious danger of obesity, with its concomitant health problems.

In all cases, what you are seeking is a good balance. Kapha dogs can be balanced by introducing a little Pitta or Vata into their lives and so on. This is only common sense. If you are cold, you seek warmth, and vice versa.

Most breeds feature a large number of dogs with double doshas. This includes most hunting, herding, and working dogs!

The classical symbol of Kapha is the calm, wise, powerful elephant, for your Kapha dog is both. They never forget, either, so they must be treated with extreme kindness. Dogs with a high percentage of Kapha include: Basset Hounds, Bulldogs, Clumber Spaniels, English Spaniels, Maltese, and Pekinese.

All dogs are good dogs. There is no "bad" or "better" dosha. The important thing is to make sure your dog stays in reasonable balance within his own natural dosha to ensure his well-being.

As everyone has observed, the weather affects both humans and dogs. It can even influence illness! Clear, cold, windy weather excites Vata. If there is already a lot of Vata present in the constitution, it overbalances it, which in turn can produce respiratory ailments and arthritis. Hot and humid weather provokes Pitta and may make dogs already overbalanced in that direction irritable or even aggressive. It can also lead to skin rashes. Gray or rainy weather exacerbates Kapha, and dogs already overbalanced in Kapha may become depressed, lethargic, or gluttonous. Some can also develop respiratory infections. (More about that in chapter 3.)

Chapter 3

The Body and Disease

Disease is the state of dis-ease, the discomforting condition of things not being "right." In other words, most disease is not natural; in fact, it's a disruption of nature. The exception is the inevitable natural breakdowns that occur through the passage of time. Disease can be physical, mental, or emotional/spiritual. For when things are not "right," all systems of the Self are affected, some subtly, some grossly. As we all know, even a slight stomachache makes us irritable or nervous, and deprives us of the power to concentrate. So whence does this dis-ease arise?

Too often, western medicine has become simply "applied pharmacology," as my holistic veterinarian, Rob Russon, explained to me. "We need to look harder for ways of treating the whole animal." Ayurveda is one such way.

In the Ayurvedic understanding of the body, there is both "gross anatomy" and a "subtle" anatomy. This subtle anatomy is comprised of *nadis,* which are invisible channels that carry the

---

Ayurveda is a growing system of medicine. It is not designed to supplant important modern advances in medicine such as vaccinations, surgery under anesthesia, and antibiotic treatment. Many medical problems, such as congenital deformities, bloat, large swallowed foreign objects, and cancerous growths, will not self-correct. However, using Ayurvedic principles will help ensure that the side effects from these powerful medicines can be reduced. In addition, the Ayurvedic emphasis on prevention will help keep your dog well. Your dog should be immunized against canine distemper, infectious canine hepatitis, canine parvovirus, rabies, and if you are boarding or showing him, kennel cough (canine infectious tracheobronchitis or Bordetella). You should also keep your dog on a regular monthly heartworm preventive and an anti-flea and tick regimen.

cosmic energy *Prana* throughout the body; *chakras,* sites of power and consciousness that help connect the spirit and the body, and *marmas* (similar to Chinese acupuncture points) which mark the intersection of vital structures (both physical and subtle).

Disease has two ways to grab hold of the individual (whether human or animal):

- *External factors* such as those brought on by seasonal change, infection, or outside pollution.
- *Internal factors* generally believed to be caused by the accumulation of toxic material within us.

These two elements are not always complctcly distinguishablc, of coursc. They inter- penetrate. One thing is well known, however. External forces have less power over a body that is pure and unpolluted, or as main-stream veterinary practitioners might say, "when the immune system is strong."

This is why a healthy lifestyle is at the heart of Ayurveda. A healthy lifestyle makes for a strong defense against disease.

Do your part in keeping your dog healthy by getting him regular check-ups, cleaning his teeth every day, grooming him carefully and often, as well as feeding him and exercising him correctly. These last two will help make sure he does not get fat, as obesity is one of the major causes of disease in dogs (people too).

Ama

One of the foci of this healing tradition is clearing out the accumulation of the physical, mental, and emotional toxins (*Ama*). The word "ama" literally means "unripe," with the implication that the toxin has not been "processed" properly by the body and is causing trouble. In Ayurvedic theory, Ama comes from improperly digested toxic particles. These can clog both the physical channels of the body (intestines, arteries, veins, and urinary tract) but also the subtle spiritual channels or *nadis* that carry the body's invisible energy. Ama also tends to collect in organs that are encased in cavities such as the cranium and abdomen. When there are excess doshas and Ama is accumulating, sickness can develop very rapidly.

*The opposite of ama is **Ojas**, the product of an efficiently operating body system (strong agni). Ojas is the "good juice" or vitality that keeps your dog running and playing and happy. It pervades all parts of the body. However, when agni is off-balance, the result of the metabolic process is ama, not ojas.*

Processing toxins requires the development of a healthy lifestyle. By feeding your dog correctly, giving him plenty of exercise, and allowing him to drink as much water as he needs, you will help keep his system flushed out and in good working order.

The ancient physician Charaka maintained that the primary cause of disease was loss of faith in God. And while dogs probably don't believe in God, they do believe in their owners and, true enough, dogs who lose faith in their owners can become despondent and ill. These are domestic animals who depend upon us to thrive, not independent wild creatures.

Because you and your dog are partners, it's important for you to take care of yourself, too. Get the rest, good food and exercise that you need, and you will find that your improved vitality and lower stress level will make a world of difference to your dog's own well-being. Dogs respond to their owners. An irritable, overworked owner brings ill-health and tension into a relationship that is supposed to be mutually nurturing.

A healthy lifestyle – for both people and dogs – means that disease is less likely to take hold in the first place; and if it does, it is more easily banished. A healthy life style is really simple: good diet, good exercise, and lowered stress. These add up to a strong body and a good attitude – the ultimate disease fighters! In some ways, it's easier to achieve a healthy diet for your dog than for yourself. Why? Because of the "willpower factor." In choosing a healthy diet for ourselves, we constantly have to struggle against the temptations of ice cream, French fries, and cheeseburgers. It's also not the easiest thing in the world to leap out of bed and hit the treadmill or gym. But with dogs it's different. Most of them glory in exercise and as for diet – well, what they don't know can't hurt them. If you never give your dog garbage, he won't yearn for it.

For dogs as well as people, one of the most difficult aspects of a healthy lifestyle is the "lowered stress" part. It may be hard for people to understand, but the modern lifestyle is also extremely stressful on our dogs in a number of ways.

First of all, dogs are naturally social animals. (By natural, I mean behavior that is inherited from their closest relatives, the wolves.) They enjoy the company of other dogs, and generally dislike being alone. It is true that through selective breeding, humans have produced some kinds of dogs who don't naturally "take" to others, such as most terriers and certain dogs bred for guarding. Some of these dogs become instead incredibly attached to their human family. Others, such as Chow Chows, are fairly aloof. Scent hounds like Beagles, on the other hand, remain very oriented to other dogs.

However, the modern dog often leads a life with little human or even canine companionship. Many dogs are "only" dogs whose owners get up at 6:00 am, leave at 7:00 and don't return for 10 to 12 hours. This is an unhappy situation for most dogs. Your dog may not be the center of your life – but you can be certain you are the center of his. A lonely life is a stressful life. Some people make the situation even worse by crating their dogs for hours every day, depriving them of the physical and mental exercise they crave. A large number of "interactive toys" and leaving the radio on to keep the dog "company" is not sufficient to ward off the incredible boredom the animal endures day after day.

Second, modern life is noisy, polluted and because of this we all pay a price in our physical and mental well-being. This isn't good for your dog either. Most dogs have little tolerance for loud street noises, although like people, they can adjust to it.

It is not possible to change everything about your dog's lifestyle all at once. Nor can you be expected to give up your day job and start working at home (although that is something to think about). Don't be afraid to start gradually – one step at a time.

A dog-walker, for instance, can do a lot to change your dog's attitude, lower his stress, and get him some exercise.

The glory of Ayurveda is that you can do so much to keep your dog healthy. This doesn't mean vets are useless – it means you'll need to consult one less often, which is good for your pocketbook and your dog's nerves.

A key element in keeping your dog healthy is prevention. This requires not only regular veterinary checkups and good home care, but also a key ingredient on your part: awareness. Awareness allows you to be sensitive to small changes in your dog's looks, behavior, or functioning that can be the very first sign of something about to go wrong. A flutter in the pulse, a minor change in appetite or bowel habits may simply reflect the normal flux of everyday living, but it might also augur a future problem.

Kinds of Disease

Ayurveda recognizes several types of disease, classified according to their causes rather than according to their manifestation or symptoms (the way in which disease is typically categorized in western medicine).

Genetic (Adibalapravritta)

In ancient time, genetic diseases such as hemophilia and so forth were considered to be due to defects in the sperm *(shukra)* or ovum *(sonata).* Little did they know back then how close they were to an understanding of modern genetics. They also understood that stress, overuse and misuse of drugs, and other elements can have harmful effects at the DNA level.

Congenital (Janmabalapravritta)

A congenital disease is one that appears at birth. It may or may not also be genetic. Some genetically controlled diseases such as Huntington's chorea in humans don't appear until later in life, while some congenital abnormalities may appear in the birth process and not be genetically transmitted to offspring. In traditional thought, congenital conditions were thought to be due to nutritional disorders and "unfulfilled cravings" of the mother. It is hard to know whether pregnant dogs have unfulfilled cravings; it's certainly possible! A natural diet should help alleviate them.

Constitutional (Doshabalapravritta)

These are the dosha diseases. Each dosha has a collection of diseases associated with it, disease which results from to much or too little of the dosha. They arise from an imbalance in any of the doshas. These diseases can also arise from an imbalance among the three Gunas (*sattva, rajas,* and *tamas*). Some of these diseases appear in the physical body, and some appear in the psychic or mental arena.

Vata dogs are in most danger of accumulating too much Vata, Kapha dogs too much Kapha, and Pitta dogs too much Pitta, which in turn can lead to the diseases associated with those specific conditions.

Traumatic (Sanghatabalapravritta)

This kind of disease includes any condition arising from trauma or accident. (The trauma can be emotional as well as physical, and be as minor as an insect bite or sharp word, or as serious as being hit by a car.)

Seasonal Influences (Klabalapravritta)

The changing seasons have an enormous effect on the accumulation, provocation, and pacification of the doshas. That doesn't mean your Pitta dog has to get sick every summer or your Kapha dog suffer during every wet, rainy period. By understanding your dog's dosha, you can take steps to modify the negative influences of your dog's "anti-weather." Proper environmental modification (a warm sweater for Vata dogs, for instance) and a correctly balanced diet can work wonders. (In some cases a normally "prohibited" spice or food ingredient might even be just the ticket.)

Vata dogs are already high in Vata, and when the fall Vata weather comes on (dry, airy, windy, and cool) the Vata dog may experience an excess of Vata and tend toward illness. If no other disease causes are present, he will probably slide through the fall with no problems, but extra stress can provoke a Vata crisis with its usual attendant problems,such as nerve irritation, flatulence, and confusion. He can also have problems when over-indulging in Vata activities like strenuous exercise.

On the other hand, a dog with low Vata in the first place tends to do better in Vata weather, which helps supply the missing elements. During hot, humid times of the year when Vata is low, a non-Vata dog may suffer a pathological decrease in Vata, resulting in nerve loss, congestion, and constipation. He may then benefit from a Vata-increasing diet, therapy, and distracting behavior.

Vata buildup often shows up as abdominal problems and gas, and in the climax stage can lead to bloat and obstruction. The early stages of Pitta buildup appears as off-color urine and appetite change. In the climax or aggravating stage it can lead to kidney, liver, and metabolic problems. Early Kapha buildup appears as lethargy and loss of appetite and later can appear as respiratory allergies and other immune problems. (Fasting is not usually a good idea in the autumn – it provokes too much Vata.)

Hot, humid weather is Pitta season. Dogs already high in Pitta become testy and aggressive during these "dog days," and experience typical Pitta-type health problems such as diarrhea and hives.

Wet weather aggravates Kapha. Therefore Kapha dogs often experience most health problems during the rainy days of early spring, including coughs and congestion problems. If this sounds like your dog, make sure you eliminate wheat, yogurt, cheese, and very cold water (and ice) from his diet. These food items tend to increase Kapha, just what you don't want, especially at this time of year.

Infectious and Spiritual (Daivabalapravritta)

This collection of ailments includes those resulting from natural traumatic events – from something as major as a hurricane to as minor as a virus. Interestingly, classical Ayurveda includes diseases arising out of "sheer jealousy" in this category. Many of the diseases in this class are transferable from one creature to another – and some of them (zoonotic diseases) can be passed from animals to humans!

Natural (Swabhavbalapravritta)

Ayurveda is wise enough to know that no being can live forever. Death is programmed into the cycle of life just as birth is. Unlike western medicine, which attempts to keep death at bay no matter what the age or condition of the patient, Ayurveda understands that death has its own hour, which should be honored. In Indian philosophy, death is not a finality, not a void, not an ending. It is the step to a higher state of existence. Natural diseases are those that occur as the body begins to break down and lose its immune powers. Treatment for these diseases is usually only palliative – the goal is to make the inevitable passing peaceful and as painless as possible.

It should be noted that the same (apparent) disease can be classified in Ayurveda in two or more different ways. Epilepsy, for example can be caused by trauma, by a drug overdose, or by an idiopathic (unknown cause). So here we have not just one disease – epilepsy – but actually several. In many cases, a subtle difference in signs can let the Ayurvedic physician know what the true cause is and therefore the most productive treatment.

Stages of Disease (Samprapti)

It is equally important to consider the various stages of disease development. In more detail, disease develops from dosha buildup in the following stages:

1. ***Sanchaya:*** the first stages of the disease, when toxins begin to accumulate and "clog" the system. Disease may first attack through the food-route, and attacks different areas of the body according to the predominant dosha. Vata tends to settle in the colon, Pitta in the small intestines, and Kapha in the stomach. This is the accumulation stage. It can occur because of diet, excess dosha, weather changes, emotional stress, or the invasion of pathogens. In Ayurvedic theory, poor digestive power and excess of one of the doshas is often responsible, and toxins collect in the gastrointestinal tract. Signs are mild and often indefinable; however, some Ayurvedic physicians can actually detect this stage in the pulse.
2. ***Prakopa:*** the second stage of the disease, in which the doshas are over-excited and cause more blockages. The cause can be improper food, exercise (or lack of it) and seasonal effects. This is the aggravation or provocation phase; generally the doshas move in an upward direction, so that Kapha, which is settled in the stomach, may express itself as vomiting, and so on.
3. ***Prasara:*** in which the toxins "overflow" the GI tract and begin to move through the body. This is the distribution phase. During this phase, getting rid of the causative agent may not be enough, as it frequently is in the first two phases. However, the disease is still completely reversible at this point.
4. ***Sthanasamsrya:*** in which the toxin finds a "weak spot" (*dhatus*) in which to settle and cause disease. This is the deposition or infiltration phase. Here degenerative disease or infection can really take hold. Malfunction or structural damage occurs, even though you may not notice it.

5. ***Vyakti:*** the first appearance of the disease itself. This is the manifestation or augmentation phase; this may be the first time that you actually notice that anything is seriously wrong with your dog. Differentiation of symptoms may appear.
6. ***Bheda:*** the most serious, chronic, or widely disseminated form of the disease. It can actually result in permanent structural or physiological damage.

The sooner you can spot and treat the disease, the more likely it is that you will be successful in eliminating it. In many cases, however, you will need the advice of a skilled Ayurvedic practitioner to catch a disease in its earliest stages. Most mainstream vets will not be able to diagnose it until the third stage at the earliest.

The Seven Vital Tissues

In Ayurvedic tradition, there are seven (*sapta*) "vital tissues" or *dhatus* in the so-called "food body" or physical body. Like the doshas, they are formed from the five elements (earth, water, fire, air, and space).

- ***Rasa:*** Plasma, cytoplasm or lymph. Its main element is water, and it provides nourishment and growth. Its main dosha is Kapha. A problem with this dhatu can result in restlessness, cardiac pain, and irritation from loud noises.
- ***Rakta:*** Blood. Its main element is fire and it provides strength and coloring. Its main dosha is Pitta. A problem with this dhatu can result in poor skin and coat.
- ***Mamsa:*** Muscle. Its main element is earth, and it provides physical strength and support for Meda (see below). Its main dosha is Kapha. A problem with this dhatu can result in emaciation.
- ***Meda:*** Fat. Its main elements are water and earth; it lubricates the body and supports Asthi (see below). Its main dosha is Kapha. A problem in this dhatu can result in bad joints.
- ***Asthi:*** Bone and cartilage. Its main elements are air and space, and it supports Mamsa and Majja. Its main dosha is Vata. A

problem in this dhatu can results in hair loss, tooth problems, and poor joints.

- ***Majja:*** Marrow and nerves. Its main element is fire; it oleates ("oils") the body and fills the Asthi. Its main dosha is Kapha. A problem with this dhatu can result in bone disease.
- ***Shukra and Artava:*** Sperm and ovum. Its main element is "refined" water; it strengthens the body and helps it reproduce. Its main dosha is Kapha. A problem with this dhatu can result in weakness and reproductive problems.

Each of these dhatus carries the karmic "memories" or experiences *(Samskaras)* that shape the body. All seven dhatus must function properly together for the health of the "Sheath of Food," or physical body. The actual term is *"Kosha,"* but it is frequently translated sheath. There is also a Sheath of Prana that activates the Sheath of Food and a Sheath of Mind at the core of both. The Dhatus support and strengthen each other – and damage to one can affect the others.

The concept of the dhatu is also applied to the plant kingdom. For instance, the juice of the leaf is the plant's "plasma," its sap or resin is its "blood," its softwood the "muscle," its gum or hard sap the "fat," its bark is the "bone," its leaf is its "marrow and nerve tissue," and its blossoms and fruits its reproductive system (something that western science and Ayurveda agree on).

The body can be thought of as a complex exchange system. It takes in air, food, and water and turns them into the seven tissues (plasma, blood, muscle, fat, bone, marrow, and eggs or sperm). It excretes via the feces, urine, and drool or sweat (in dogs mainly through the footpads). These are the Three Wastes *(Mala),* produced by the dhatus, and like everything else are composed of the five elements (earth, water, fire, air, and space).

Purisa, or feces, is the waste remaining after nutrients from digested food have been absorbed in the small intestine, and transferred elsewhere. The large intestine takes up most of the remaining water and salt and expels the rest as fecal material.

Mutra, or urine, is produced by the renal system – the kidneys, bladder and urethra. This system also regulates the fluid balance and maintains blood pressure.

Sweda or sweat (perhaps you can see the etymological connection) passes through the skin pores; it controls body temperature and helps to regulate the electrolytic balance. Dogs don't sweat much (they can through their pawpads, though) and the primary sweda fluid for dogs occurs through panting and drooling and serves much the same purpose.

Modern Ayurvedic practitioners often add a fourth waste product, carbon dioxide.

To stay in good health, the body must eliminate the mala in the proper amount and with the correct frequency. (Females also produce milk for their offspring, but this issuance is obviously not waste, but a vital nutrient for the new life the mother has borne.)

The goal of Ayurveda is to maintain a healthy balance of the Seven Tissues, Three Wastes, Three Doshas, as well as the Body, Mind, and Senses. When they are in correct balance, a state of health, called *Swastha* (totally happy in oneself) is the result. When they are not in balance, the powerful biological fire called Agni is stilled or overheated; the breath (Vayu) is altered, the liquids within the body (Jal) dry up or flood, and the earth or bodily structure (Prithvi) itself falters. Eventually, the whole encompassing being and its environment (Akash) is threatened.

In Ayurvedic thought, male animals have several "gates," or openings in the body. These gates include the openings for the five senses (visual, auditory, gustatory, olfactory and tactile) which are traditionally located in the head (although we know that the tactile sense is everywhere present), plus the urethra and anus. Female animals have the vagina and the nipples in addition. Male animals have nipples too, of course, but they are non-functioning.

It seems complex, and to some extent it is. Luckily, however, the Self is infinitely wise, and manages to balance most of these automatically. Just as when you are walking, you don't consciously have to think about how to put each foot down. If you twist your ankle on a stone, however, you may have to relearn much of what used to come naturally.

In Ayurveda, disease itself is a stumbling block. And though the Self manages remarkably well to keep a steady course despite cross winds of disease-causing organisms, bad food, and poor exercise, sometimes it gets overwhelmed. At this point, it may be time to trim the sails and plot a new course.

Anything that "gums up" the works contributes to disease. Lack of exercise does not allow the lungs to breathe deeply enough to expel its toxins; overeating can overload the stomach, the accumulation of plaque on teeth can eventually result in bacteria in the bloodstream. At this point the body becomes a *beej-bhoomi,* a seeding ground (or as westerners might say a "breeding ground") for the development of toxins, or Ama.

Ama: *The Root Cause*

In Ayurvedic thought, the chief cause of disease is Ama, a product that forms when enzyme activity decreases or when food is not properly digested. (It can sometimes be noticed as a coating on the tongue.) Ama can be caused by a buildup of toxins from excess dosha or from a bacterial or viral invasion. Resembling a kind of sludge, Ama can lodge in various places in the body, obstructing channels (*Srotas* – the word actually means "path" or "highway) and causing disease." Each Srota has a "root," and "passage," and an "opening." Srotas include the intestines, arteries, veins, and uterus. Even the mind is said to have srotas! There are also even more subtle channels called *Chakras.*

Purifying the Body

Indian physicians have long recognized the importance of cleanliness, both internal and external. It is just as important for dogs are for people, and it is traditional to initiate a cleansing routine to prevent and cure illness. Typically, such a routine lasts for about a week. During the 5–7 days of a home cleansing period, keep your dog on a light, natural diet. Be especially careful not to feed food loaded with preservatives and other additives.

Begin with Oleation (Snehana)

One standard way to clear Ama from the body is to begin with a treatment called *internal oleation.* The general effect of oleation is to create an effect of fluidity, moistness, and softness, and is best used for diseases that produce the opposite effects. Traditional

Indian practitioners use clarified butter, or *ghee* (see chapter 5 for information about ghee), but it is also acceptable to use flaxseed oil. For this procedure give your dog one tablespoon of flaxseed oil three times a day for three days. You can simply put it in his food or in warm milk. Flaxseed oil is especially beneficial to Pitta dogs. Add just a pinch of rock salt to the ghee or flaxseed oil for Vata dogs. For Kapha dogs, add just a pinch of ginger, black pepper, and *pippali* (Indian long pepper). This is called *trikatu,* which is one of the ten traditional herb mixtures and is often prescribed for colds, flu and the like. If pippali is unavailable, it can be omitted. For Pitta dogs, give the ghee or flaxseed oil plain.

Follow with Massage (External oleation)

After the three days of oleation, follow with 10 minutes of gentle massage once a day for 5 – 7 days. With humans, oil is used for the whole body, but unless you have a Chinese Crested, American Hairless Terrier, Peruvian Inca Orchid Dog or a similar breed, it is best to use only a little oil on the belly, paws, or other hairless area, carefully wiping it off afterwards. For Vata dogs use sesame oil, for Pittas used sunflower oil, and for Kaphas use corn oil.

It may also be of benefit to give your dog 1/4 to half a teaspoon of the Triphala – the three herbs (see chapter 5). This is gentle cleanser with a slight laxative effect.

Another way to help purify the body of toxin is through the use of blood-cleansing herbs like burdock.

The best way to purify thc body of your pet is through the gentle methods of "palliation" and "pacification," which relies on herbal treatment. Indian herbs are the most traditional, but more readily available western herbs have similar effects. It is best to avoid using Chinese herbs in Ayurveda, as their purity is often in

---

Traditional Indian therapy also includes a practice called vamana or therapeutic vomiting which, along with certain other practices, should be undertaken only under the strict guidance of a Vaidya, or Ayurvedic physician. However, the dog's body seems wiser that ours, as dogs frequently know when to purge themselves. While it has always been a mystery to western medicine as to exactly why dogs eat grass, the Ayurvedic practitioner understands the reason – to assist in a purge of unhealthy Ama. Dogs are gifted with the ability to purge themselves quite easily and without any fuss.

question. In addition, many Chinese herbs seem to be more dangerous to use than Indian or Western herbs.

Diseases have psychological and karmic as well as physical causes. The more complex the animal is the more likely it is that psychological causes play a part in the development of the disease. Simple creatures like lightning bugs and clams probably have few psychological issues. Even complex animals like wolves, which live in a free, natural environment, probably experience little abnormal stress. Domesticated animals such as dogs, cats and horses (but especially dogs) are different. They live intimately with us, and have chosen to share our lives – and our stresses.

Like most good medical practice, Ayurvedic medicine goes after the causes of the disease; it doesn't merely attempt to relieve symptoms.

In Ayurveda, it's believed that most disease results from misuse of the bodily or mental senses (which includes insufficient or over exercise), poor diet, or inattention to the correct life style for the season or to one's age.

In the Ayurvedic tradition, the material self is composed of five increasingly subtle bodies, or layers:

- The Food Body (*Annamaya*): it is sustained by food
- The Air and Space Body (*Pranamaya*): it is sustained by breath
- The Mind Body (*Manomaya*): it is sustained by the individual mind
- The Intelligence Body (*Vijnanamya*): it is sustained by universal mind
- The Bliss Body (*Anandamaya*): it is sustained by the infinite wholeness of the cosmos.

The Ayurvedic physician is called the Vaidya. *The name comes from the Sanskrit word "vid," meaning knowledge or vision. Hence the vaidya is indeed one who "knows." In India, the home of Ayurvedic medicine, the vaidya's course of training lasts for six years, and involves eight specialties: internal medicine, pediatrics, psychiatry, eye/ear/nose/throat, toxicology, geriatrics, and fertility/sexuality. However, the dog or animal owner also has a critical role to play. Note: please be aware that not every practitioner offering services or treatments called "Ayurvedic" has been trained in an Ayurvedic medical school so it is always important to check credentials. There is no licensing for the practice of Ayurvedic medicine in the United States.*

The food body or *Annamaya* is rooted in earth and water. As the most physical of all the elements and shared equally by all beings, it is the closest connection between animals, the Earth, and human beings. The more damage we do to our Earth, the more deleterious the effects will be to the food bodies of the animals, plants and people who live on it. Our food bodies cannot thrive or even survive for long upon a decimated planet. And while the more subtle parts of our beings do not need food in an ultimate sense, it is absolutely necessary for life on this earth. The food body contains the primal elements of earth and water – water for our birth and earth to support us. Both are equally necessary and both must be kept pure.

The *Pranamaya* is the second layer of the material self. It contains our memories, desires, predilections, and emotions. This part of existence is also shared by all sentient creatures, although it is weaker in amoebas than in dogs or human beings.

The third layer is the Mindbody or *Manomaya,* representing the individual mind or mental abilities. It is represented by fire, the bright sparkling sign of intelligence. All living forms have an individual mind, but this mind is more highly developed in humans than in dogs. This explains why humans can read *Hamlet* and dogs can't, although there's no guaranteeing that either species necessarily can understand it.

Vijnanamaya or the Intelligence Body is the fourth layer. In this case, intelligence does not refer to the individual, but to the universal order of the cosmos. It is this universal order that controls the seasons, the life cycles, and the laws of physics. While all creatures participate in the working of the cosmos, on this earth at least, it appears that only human beings can glimpse how it works. For example, all animals can digest food. Only human beings can understand how the digestion system works, and most of us aren't really too sure how it works either.

The fifth layer is *Anandamaya* or Bliss body. It fills and fulfills the universe. It is so subtle is cannot be grasped, yet because of its subtlety it is everywhere. Not one subatomic particle on earth is devoid of Anandamaya. The great goal of human endeavor is to realize it.

Stress and Disease

We all know that stress causes disease. How that stress manifests itself depends largely on the dog's particular doshas (remembering always that more than one dosha can be at work).

Stressed Vata dogs tend towards anxiety and phobias. These may result in colitis and other disorders. Stressed Pitta dog tends to become angry and aggressive. And stressed Kapha dogs tend to respond by eating more and more, often with very unfortunate results.

Ayurvedic Disease Management: Chikitsa

The veterinarian skilled in Ayurveda often follows a phased plan in diagnosing and treating a patient. Obviously, if the diagnosis is not correct, the treatment will be wrong as well. Good diagnosis is a fine art, and while you can sometimes successfully identify your dog's condition, you could also be wrong. And so can your vet, Ayurvedic practitioner, or anyone else. One hundred percent accuracy is only a dream. However, careful observation, questioning and, in many cases testing, will very likely give you a good diagnosis.

The most important part of the diagnosis starts with you, before you ever see your vet. You know your dog. By carefully observing changes in his behavior (and taking note of them) you will be your veterinarian's best assistant.

The Home Health Check

Since ama can interfere with a dog's system on several levels, during your home health check, take time to examine each element. It is an excellent idea to check your dog once a week. The best way to begin is by examining his normal functions. As you become more acquainted with Ayurvedic methods, you will discover just how much you can learn from this sort of checkup.

Activity Level: A drop in normal activity level could indicate a serious problem. Be able to assess his capacity for work and exercise.

Appetite: Dogs, especially Kapha dogs, are programmed to be hungry most of the time. A reduced appetite may be the first sign of a toxic buildup. It may often indicate the depression that accompanies many illnesses, including fever and any disease producing nausea. A bad tooth may also cause a decrease in appetite. In the same way, a sudden, unexplained increase in appetite or a "depraved" appetite may also indicate problems. Increased appetite could mean Cushing's disease, diabetes mellitus, or exocrine pancreatic insufficiency, all Kapha diseases. Dogs on corticosteroids are also often very hungry.

Breathing: The average resting respiratory rate for a healthy dog is 10 to 30 breaths per minute, so you can count breaths for 15 seconds and multiply by four. The breath should be steady and unrestricted. Labored breathing can indicate pneumonia, heart failure, anemia, fluid in or around the lungs, or even diaphragmatic hernia. Accompanied by a cough, it could mean kennel cough, bronchitis, or heartworm. Constant panting may also indicate a problem including Cushing's disease or pain. Dogs on corticosteroids may also pant. (A dog can pant up to 200 times per minute!)

Ears: Check for ear mites, redness, and debris. Flop-eared dogs are prone to waxy buildup and infections.

Emotions: Ama can be emotional as well as physical. The basic question to ask is: Does your dog seem happy? Do you provide a stable, loving environment for your pet? Do you have a strong bond with him? Do you spend enough time with him? Knowing your dog's basic dosha will help you understand when something goes wrong. The normally placid Kapha plunges into lethargy, the energetic and focused Pitta gets aggressive, and the energetic Vata becomes flighty.

Eyes: Eyes should be full of shine and luster. Squinting, swelling, redness, opacity, and apparent pain can mean trouble. Watery eyes indicate too much Kapha, while red eyes may suggest too much Vata or Pitta. Excessive blinking may be a sign of fear or nervousness. Yellow conjunctiva may suggest a weak liver.

Feces: Your dog should eliminate once or twice a day with firm (but not rock hard) stools. Constipation or diarrhea may both be signs of problems. Excessively smelly feces can be a sign of parvovirus or other diseases. Vata aggravated feces tend to be hard, dry and grayish. Excess Pitta can turn feces liquid and excess Kapha may produce mucus-coated feces.

Joints and Movement: Your dog should move freely on well-lubricated joints. "Dry" dogs like Vata animals are particularly low in lubrication, so are most likely to be affected by stiffening joints.

Mouth and Gums: Breath and teeth should be clean and the gums pink. Simply lift the skin around the canine tooth and have a look. Pale, dark red, blue or purple gums may indicate trouble. (There are a few breeds, of course, whose normal gum color is purple or black. In that case you should check the eyelids.) A difficulty in examining your dog's mouth may indicate a tooth problem, as may a swelling right below the eye (possibly an abscessed carnassial tooth).

Nails: Dry and brittle nails can be a sign of disease; they are most common in Vata type dogs.

Nose: A wet cold nose doesn't necessarily mean a healthy dog, any more than a dry one means a sick one. But the nose can provide some important health clues. A discharge from the nose, whether bloody, mucus-like, or purulent can signal disease. Your vet can sometimes figure out the problem by flushing out the nose and examining the fluid, but often the dog will need to be sedated or anesthetized to get a clearer picture. Possible problems can include a nasal tumor, infection, clotting problem, or broken blood vessel.

Pulse: You can learn how to take a pulse Ayurvedically. While it's best to learn under the tutelage of an experience Vaidya, the fundamentals are fairly easy to understand and although you probably will not be able to use the pulse to make a diagnosis, you can learn more than you might think. A pulse occurs with every heart beat. So the pulse rate and heart rate are the same. In traditional Ayurvedic practice, the best time to take a pulse is in the early morning, before the dog has had breakfast, but after it has eliminated. Do not take the pulse after strenuous exercise, or if the dog has a fever.

For male animals, take the pulse on the right leg. For females, take the pulse on the left leg. You can take the pulse on your dog's chest just below the elbow joint, but sometimes you can get a better pulse by feeling it high in the inside of the thigh where the leg joins the body. That is called the "femoral pulse." The normal pulse for a dog ranges from 70 to 180 beats per minute, with Vata pulses on the higher end of that scale and Kapha pulses at the lower end. You can take the pulse for 15 seconds and multiply by four. Don't be alarmed if the pulse rate seems to change. The pulse will be faster when the dog breathes in and slower when he breathes out. This is perfectly normal and even has a fancy name: sinus arrhythmia.

In Ayurveda, the pulse is taken with three fingers. The forefinger feels for the energy generated by ordinary circulation and respiration, the second detects metabolic activity, and the ring finger checks for structural health supported by the muscles, bones, and joints. When Vata is strong in the constitution, the index finger will feel a strong, irregular beat that moves in waves like the motion of a serpent. This type of pulse is called a "snake pulse." If the pulse is felt most strongly in the middle finger, this is the Pitta pulse, which is an excited, jumping-around-like-a-frog pulse. It is indeed called a "frog pulse." The ring finger is most attuned to Kapha or a "swan pulse," which is a slow, floating sort of pulse. The kind of pulse you feel will indicate what doshas are most active.

Skin and Coat: Should be clean, supple, and free from sores, lumps, and infections. A Vata aggravated skin tends to be coarse, rough and cool to the touch; skin overbalanced in the Pitta direction feel hot and moist; cold skin indicates too much Kapha.

Temperature: Ancient Ayurvedic physicians had no accurate way to measure temperature, but contemporary ones do not shun a thermometer! The correct rectal temperature for a dog is about 101°F, although it can range from 99°F to 102.5°F. Other signs of a feverish condition such as a hot skin and dry nose may be ancillary proofs.

Thirst: Excessive water consumption is a sign of many illnesses, including diabetes mellitus or insipidus, kidney failure, liver disease, high blood calcium, and so on.

Tongue: The tongue can also reveal volume to a skilled observer. A dry, rough, blackish tongue suggest an over-balance in the Vata direction, an overly red tongue can suggest too much Pitta (and is classic sign of heat stroke), and a whitish, slimy, coated tongue indicates too much Kapha.

Urine: Urine is collected via a free-catch method into a clean glass container. Normal urine should be comparatively odor free and light-colored. Variations such as the following, signal an imbalance among the doshas: Vata urine is pale yellow, with an "oily" constituency; Pitta urine is an intense yellow or reddish.

Kapha urine is white, foamy, or muddy. Very dilute, watery urine may indicate a problem. Dogs who have problems urinating or who suddenly seem to be urinating more than usual may have a medical condition. (See thirst, above.) Certain drugs may also have this effect. In traditional Ayurvedic medicine, a drop or so of sesame oil is added to the urine to see which doshas may be at work: a "snakelike" form indicates Vata; an umbrella shaped one suggest Pitta, and a pearl shaped drop represents Kapha.

Voice: Your dog's bark can tell you a lot about his condition, especially when there is a change in quality, volume or frequency. Ayurvedic medicine makes a big deal out of hearing the voice.

Seeing the Ayurvedic Practitioner

Correct Ayurvedic practice stands firmly upon three "legs": textual knowledge *(aptopadesa),* direct perception *(pratyaksha)* and inference *(anumana).* Each has role in the detection, understanding, and treatment of disease. Together, they make up the "Threefold Examination" or *Tribidha Pariksha.*

In the old days, textual knowledge depended upon knowledge of the sacred texts. This is verbal testimony *(Shabda).* While shabda is still considered critical, especially for emotional and mental disorders, the modern vaidya has a broader interpretation of the term *aptopadesa.* This includes objective reports such as x-rays, blood tests, and ultrasound. There is no point in treating bladder stones, for instance, if x-rays indicate that no bladder stones are present!

The second part of the exam is the part most visible to the patient, the direct examination. In Ayurveda, the first examination is done with the eyes and ears alone. The vaidya takes note of the animal's coat condition, eyes, tongue, general build, bone structure, and posture. It may also include a fecal examination and urinalysis or urine culture. He may chat with you, but his main work at this point is observation. He will carefully note the interactions between you and your dog. This part of the exam is called *Darshana* – looking.

The second part of the exam – *Sparsha,* is the touching part of the exam. It usually begins with pulse taking, as described earlier, but in great, sensitive depth. The Ayurvedic practitioner can learn enormous amounts from this simple action, as Ayurveda teaches that the circulatory system carries around more than blood. It's also an important conduit for energy and the life force.

Deeper pressure results in detecting deeper, more varied physiological activity. This may seem very odd to a western practitioner who is trained to rely mostly upon instruments. However, the human fingers are all ancient physicians had, and they "fine-tuned" them to detect the many secrets hidden in the pulse. There is nothing magical about this, but it does take years of experience and a sensitive touch. At first you can't expect to extract the same information that a vaidya might; but you can practice over and over with healthy dogs and with sick ones, to learn what the pulse is saying.

Then comes the serious questioning or *Prashna,* in which the vaidya will ask you a series of questions about the dog. You may think some of them unrelated to the symptoms displayed but be patient.

All of these procedures are designed to reveal the patient's basic constitution *(prakriti),* as well as the vikruti, or current altered state of the Doshas.

Doctors also use inference *(anumana)* and comparison *(upamana)* in analyzing a diseased state. They compare the present condition of the dog with past condition, and make an inference between the overt symptom and the disease it manifests.

The next step is to discover the cause of the problems, and if possible remove them. Sometimes, of course this is not possible. If the dog is ill because of genetic problems, or is allergic to a multitude of things, the cause cannot be removed. (That does not mean there is no hope; it just means that the simplest, most direct method of dealing with the disease is not possible.) However, other causes may well factor into disease onset, factors that can be altered. These may include diet, lifestyle, stress, and so on.

Treatment may consist of mainstream veterinary care, nutritional changes, herbal cures, massage, or even pranayana (breathing exercises) or yoga work for the owner as a step to relieving stress. Often, a detoxification program is initiated. This detoxification can be of two types. The first type is elimination (*panchakarma* or the "five actions"), a rigorous procedure that should be undertaken only by a veterinarian skilled in Ayurveda, and many of the techniques (such as blood letting) have been modified to fit the findings of modern science.

A better choice for most animal conditions, and the only option for pet owners – is the more conservative palliation or *shamana*. After the body is detoxified, the practitioner may prescribe a program to rejuvenate the body and boost the immune system. Some therapies are designed to pacify the aggravated dosha, others target the disease more specifically.

Your Dog's Feelings

Animals have emotions just as human beings do. In fact, because they lack the intellect to control these emotions, you might even say that animals are more emotional than people. Dogs are pack animals and get *lonely* when left by themselves. They get *bored* if not given exercise or a specific job to do. They become *tense* or *distressed* when screamed at or physically punished. Every one of these emotions is damaging to his health and harmful to your relationship with him. Your dog's emotional health is just that – HEALTH. You can feed your dog the best diet in the world and take him to the vet regularly, but if he is ignored, bored, or stressed, he will get sick – and so might you.

In Ayurvedic thought, any cruelty or unnecessary harshness to animals damages your own soul – and karma insures that you will suffer for it yourself, either in this life or in the next one. That's just the way things are.

Chapter 4

Food

"I am food. I am the consumer of food. I eat the consumer of foods. I consume the whole universe."
Taittiriya Upanishad (11.96)

"Aaharah pranah!"
Food is life

These words alone are enough to show how important food is in Ayurvedic medicine!

Why Diet Is So Important

In Indian philosophy, what supports the body? Food and breath, as they are the basis for keeping us in homeostatic balance. The perfect Ayurvedic diet not only nourishes the body, but also maintains or restores the proper balance of the doshas. In this chapter we'll concentrate on food and diet, and in chapter 7 we'll focus on exercise.

When correctly supported (food) and correctly exercised (breath) the body maintains its balance in the universe. A disease means imbalance. For example, an ingested element can act as a food to nourish the system, a medicine to balance the system, or as a poison to disturb the system. The same element may act in more than one of these roles, depending on circumstances and the state of the system. What may be healthful to one dosha can be damaging to another, and can also change with the season.

In Ayurveda, the distinction between food and medicine is not as rigid as it is in the western understanding of these terms.

Diet is also important in that when you feed a diet that is in accordance with your dog's basic nature, if he does get sick, medications will work better. Dogs fed an improper diet have just as much trouble assimilating medicines as they do food.

In modern terms, eating incompatible food may release free radicals in the body.

Different foods have different effects upon the different doshas. For example, some foods tend to aggravate Vata. Therefore, a dog already tending strongly in the Vata direction is usually best off not eating those foods, especially in "Vata-weather" – those cool, dry, windy days that predominate in autumn, although of course they can occur at other times. Other foods aggravate Pitta and have most effect in the hot, humid "dog days of summer." These foods are best not fed to dogs already overbalanced in the Pitta direction. And certain other foods provoke Kapha, especially during the wet, rainy days that tend to pop up in spring.

One who follows Ayurvedic theory knows that while a rose is a rose is rose, a potato might be a potato and then again it might not be. In finding the best diet for your dog (or yourself, for that matter) you need consider not only the intrinsic quality of the food, but how those qualities can be altered by cooking or in combination with other foods. The quantity of the food, the climate, the season, or even the time of day when it is eaten, can all have subtle but far reaching effects. Most of these effects are slight but cumulative. This doesn't mean that if you give your dog the "wrong" food for a few days, weeks, or even months, he will keel over and die (unless you are actively poisoning him), but it does mean that keeping to a general Ayurvedic plan devised for your dog and the season will keep him generally in good shape. He may still get sick, but proper nutrition prepares him to fight off the sickness. It also provides a way to his recovery.

The weather has an increasing effect when it comes along in "spells." An occasional rainy day doesn't have too much provoking effect on Kapha, but when it rains for a week, the effect is aggravated.

Diet and the Three Gunas

Like everything else, different foods are inhabited by different proportions of the three gunas. Foods which include a lot of *sattva* (the guna of mental clarity and perception) include fresh dairy and butter, fresh vegetables, and sprouted grains. They tend to be "sweet," in the Ayurvedic sense of the term (see below). *Rajasic* foods (the guna of energy) for dogs are energy giving; many are strongly flavored. Meat is a rajasic food for dogs (but not for people). *Tamasic* foods (the guna of unconsciousness) include processed meat, as well as any foods that are stale or spoiled.

Agni

In Ayurvedic theory, Agni is the digestive fire that controls not simply digestion, but indeed all aspects of metabolism. (Actually there are thirteen different kinds of Agni, but the most important one is the digestive fire, *jatharagni.*) Agni is necessary for every tissue. It is considered acidic in nature, and helps destroy destructive organisms in the system. It is closely connected to, but not identical with, Pitta. Some Ayurvedic theorists make the connection by saying that Agni is the content, while Pitta is the container. Agni is also related to Vata, which controls the subtle movements of material and energy throughout the body. There is a saying in Ayurveda that one is only as old as his Agni.

The Six Tastes (Rasas)

The basic principle in Ayurvedic eating is to balance the three doshas, which may mean eating less of the foods towards which your dog "naturally" inclines, as they may make him sick. For Ayurvedic purposes, foods are divided into six classes: *sweet, salty, sour, bitter, pungent,* and *astringent.* Most foods combine two or more tastes. I am including examples here only of what your dog is likely to consume (whether or not you want him to).

Western science tells us that there are only four tastes: sweet, sour, salty, and bitter. The Ayurvedic "astringent'; and "pungent" are subtle combinations of these. Dogs can taste the same tastes as humans, although their response to bitter is ambivalent. (Cats, on the other hand, are unable to taste "sweet," which is why they don't usually bother eating cake.) While in humans, the taste buds are all over the tongue (with different types clustered in different spots), in canines, the taste buds are clumped together in papillae along the rear two-thirds of the tongue, although some are present in soft palate and even in the throat, possible accounting for the way dogs tend to "gulp" their food. Each taste bud is a little tunnel that contains up to 50 "taste receptors." Interestingly, the most common taste buds in the dog's mouth are the so-called Group A and D taste buds which have a strong response to natural sugars like fructose and glucose. Saccharin tastes "bitter" not sweet to dogs. Another sugar substitute, xylitol, commonly found in sugarless chewing gum, is toxic to them. The evolutionary explanation for this is that their liking for sweets helped primitive dogs survive when game was scarce. Ayurvedic medicine also classified meat as among the "sweet" tastes. Dogs appear to be able to "taste" water and other inorganic substances, which people are unable to do.

- ***Sweet:*** The sweet taste comes from Earth and Water. It is easily the most dominant taste, and produces its most profound effect upon the pancreas and spleen. All carbohydrates, sugars, fats, and amino acids contain some "sweet" taste. Examples include meats, ghee (clarified butter), egg yolks, goat's milk, most grains, carrots, sweet potatoes, rice, wheat, pasta, potatoes, peas, butter, sugary foods and syrups. Even water is considered "sweet." Sweet spices include basil, licorice root, red cloves, peppermint, slippery elm, and fennel. Sweet foods are considered to be oily, cooling, and heavy. Sweet foods increase the vital essence, and are especially good for the skin and coat. They raise Kapha and decrease (or balance) Vata and Pitta. Excessive amounts of sweet food aggravate typical Kapha disorders such as obesity, lymphatic congestions, coughs, and diabetes. Vata and Pitta types need more sweet foods than do Kapha types. Highly processed sweets like candy should be avoided (and your dog shouldn't eat them, either). Emotionally, sweet tastes produce a sense of contentment and pleasure.
- ***Salty:*** The salty taste comes from Water and Fire. It produces its most profound effects on the kidneys. The salty taste is needed by all dogs, but more by Vata types. Salty foods are all processed foods as well as kelp and salt itself, of course. Watery vegetables also contain high amounts of salt. Most dogs eating processed food already get more salt in their diet than they

need. Salt is considered to be *heating, oily,* and *heavy.* It clears channels from obstructions and cleanses the tissues. Moderate use of salt decreases (balances) Vata and increases Pitta and Kapha. Salty foods may lessen colon pain and keep electrolyte balance. It is antispasmodic. Too much salt can aggravate Pitta and Kapha, and thicken the blood, induce water retention, and be bad for the skin and coat. On the other hand, in proper amounts, the salty taste tends to calm nerves and lessen anxiety.

- ***Sour:*** The sour taste comes from Earth and Fire, and it produces its most profound effects on the liver. This is the taste of adventure, and is needed in small amounts by every dosha, but is most helpful for Vatas. Examples include organic acids and fermented foods such as yogurt, butter, sour cream, and cheese, especially hard cheese. Sour spices are coriander, caraway, and cloves. Sour qualities are liquidity, lightness, heating, and oiliness. Sour decreases (balances) Vata and increases Pitta and Kapha. Pitta dogs should be given sour foods only in the tiniest amounts. When used correctly in the diet, sour foods stimulate the appetite, help heart function, and ameliorate many digestive disorders, including gas. Sour foods are also said to sharpen the mind. However, excess use of the sour taste is bad for the skin and coat, and can cause problems in the throat, chest, heart, bladder, and urethra. Emotionally, the sour tastes awaken both the mind and the senses.
- ***Bitter:*** The bitter taste comes from Air and Space. It produces its most profound effects on the heart. It is considered a "medicinal taste," and is a good general toner. It is present in leafy greens like broccoli and dandelion greens, and in many alkaloids and glycosides (these aren't normal foods, but cause the bitter taste). The average American diet is sparse on bitter tastes, one reason that broccoli (although it is so good for us) is rather famous for being disliked, especially by children. Unlike the sweet taste, bitter needs to be cultivated and requires a more sophisticated palate. Bitter is present in the spice turmeric and is cool, light, and dry. Bitter aggravates Vata and decreases (balances) Pitta and Kapha. It is most important to Pitta dogs, however. This is one of the most healing tastes. Bitter herbs, such as celery, watercress, chicory, yellow dock, fenugreek, dandelion root, are classic blood cleansers, and they also help

clear the senses. Too much of them, however, can cause dizziness and dehydration.

- ***Pungent/Spicy:*** The pungent taste comes from Fire and Air. It produces its most profound effect upon the lungs. It is present in peppers, garlic, ginger and most spices. It is also present in volatile oils. This taste is best for Kapha types, and should be used only in the tiniest amounts by Pittas and to an even lesser extent by Vatas. It decreases Kapha. It stimulates the appetite, and is considered to be heating, light, and dry. Used correctly, it improves digestion and aids circulation by clearing the channels. It is good for the mind too. Overuse can cause general debility, irritation, back pain, and diarrhea. The pungent taste opens the mind.
- ***Astringent:*** The astringent taste comes from Air and Earth. It produces its most profound effects on the colon. This is another medicinal taste. It is cooling, drying, and heavy. Like bitter, astringent tastes increase Vata and decrease (balance) Pitta and Kapha. Examples include beans, cranberries, parsley, lentils, and most raw vegetables. It is also found in foods high in tannin such as apple cider, allspice, turmeric, and cinnamon. (Most herbal products contain tannin.) It cleans the blood and helps the heart. It can also help diarrhea and slow down bleeding. Immoderate use can include neuromuscular disorders. The astringent taste cools passions.

All mammals need the six tastes every day, but the amount eaten should ideally balance the dominant doshas.

In a Nutshell:

To increase Vata:	Pungent, bitter, astringent
To decrease Vata:	Sweet, sour, salty
To increase Pitta:	Pungent, sour, salty
To decrease Pitta:	Sweet, bitter, astringent
To increase Kapha:	Sweet, sour, salty
To decrease Kapha:	Pungent, bitter, astringent.

Or to put it another way:

- Sweet reduces Vata and Pitta and increases Kapha.
- Sour reduces Vata, but increases Pitta and Kapha.

- Salty reduces Vata, but increases Pitta and Kapha.
- Pungent reduces Kapha, but increases Pitta and Vata.
- Bitter reduces Pitta and Kapha, but increases Vata.
- Astringent reduces Pitta and Kapha, but increases Vata.

In the Ayurvedic view, foods cause a chain taste response or "taste cascade." The first taste is the immediate flavor on the tongue, called *rasa,* referring on one of the six tastes. The second phase of the "taste" process is *virya,* the heating or cooling effect during digestion, as the food moves through the body. Pungent, sour, and salty foods are considered heating. Bitter, astringent, and sweet foods are considered cooling. Bitter foods are the most cooling, and pungent foods the most heating. The third, post-digestive phase is *vipaka,* in which the foods resolve into their final effect upon the body.

Sweet, pungent, and sour tastes remain essentially unchanged throughout the process. However, salty food becomes sweet in its final effect, while bitter and astringent foods become pungent.

In addition, there are exceptions. Honey is considered warming rather than cooling like most other sweets. And onions change from pungent to sweet when they are cooked. (We use onions merely as a well-known example. Don't feed dogs onions. Even a quarter cup of onions can result in a severe although temporary hemolytic anemia in dogs.)

Taste is not the only quality affecting a food effect upon the body. The food's temperature and texture have equally powerful influences. Cooking food usually modifies their effect. In general, Ayurvedic foods should be cooked to prevent their effect from being too sudden and harsh.

Tastes (Rasas) *and Qualities of Various Foods*

Meat

Ayurveda requires that humans consume vegetarian foods, rather than meat-based meals. This is partly for health reasons, and partly because Ayurveda knows that food that comes from suffering and dying has a karmic impact on the consumer. Animals, however, are free from this burden. Animals cannot create more karma; they have no moral decisions to make. Animals can only work out the karma they have. Dogs, descended from wolves, are omnivores with a decided predilection for meat. In addition, meat is considered the most nourishing of foods, with a higher "biologic value" than vegetables, meaning that for dogs, meat is more completely turned into foods that the body can use.

In the Ayurvedic world, meat is said to be heavy and of sweet taste, although the white meat of chicken has a secondary astringent quality, and duck has a secondary pungent quality. All meat (except buffalo) has a heating quality, whereas buffalo meat is considered cooling. This applied originally to water buffalo; it is unclear as to whether the same is true for bison, the "American buffalo."

Meat is the main protein source for dogs, and most dogs require about 20 percent high- quality protein in their diet. High-quality protein translates as protein that comes from meat, dairy, or eggs, not from vegetables. Even though corn, for example, does have protein, it is "incomplete" and must be balanced by another vegetable protein source to be complete. A complete protein contains adequate amounts of all the essential amino acids (essential amino acids are ones that dogs cannot make on their own). Very few vegetables, other than soybeans (to which many dogs are allergic or intolerant), have a complete protein profile. On the other hand, all meats offer complete protein, and do not differ from each other in the quality of that protein.

Since even sweet-loving Kaphas and hot-blooded Pittas need meat, it is better for them to eat the "cooler" meats such as venison, and to a lesser extent, chicken and turkey rather than beef or lamb. Vata dogs, on the other hand, often do better with beef and lamb.

- ***Beef***: Reduces Vata and increase Pitta and Kapha. Its taste is considered sweet and its effect warming. However, since Ayurveda is a system developed in India, beef is generally frowned on. However, beef is generally acknowledged as a nutritious blood and muscle-building substance and good where strength and endurance are required.
- ***Chicken and Turkey:*** Easier to digest than other meats; both white and dark meat are both considered sweet and warming. However, white meat is said to reduce Pitta and Kapha and dark meat raises them. On the other hand, white meat increases Vata, and dark meat lowers it.

- ***Duck:*** More nutritious but harder to digest that chicken or turkey. It is sweet, pungent, and warming. It lowers Vata and increases Pitta and Kapha.
- ***Lamb and Pork:*** Both considered sweet and warming, raising all three doshas. Pork traditionally has an extremely high fat content, which makes it heavy and difficult to digest.
- ***Venison:*** Astringent, pungent, and cooling. It reduces Vata and raises Pitta and Kapha.

Fish is considered sweet, salty (ocean fish) and warming. It reduces Vata and increases Pitta and Kapha. Fish should be fresh and steamed or baked.

In India the cow is a sacred animal. Interestingly, only the cow, not the bull or steer has this sacred status, so beef from steers is preferable. Most high quality beef intended for people does come from steers; however, the dog food market is more likely to make use of cow-beef, as the source is often aged or no longer milk-producing cows.

While it is possible to make a dog into a vegetarian by providing carefully balanced vegetable proteins and, ideally, dairy and eggs, dogs are really designed to eat meat. It is part of the karma they have inherited. The classic (and complex) human Ayurvedic diet must be revised for dogs.

In like manner, dogs do not have the finely tuned taste buds that people have developed. They like to eat almost anything, including garbage, as well as food that is definitely not good for them – like chocolate. (In some ways they are very much like American teenagers!)

Certain combinations are contraindicated in the Ayurvedic tradition. It is not recommended, for instance, to combine milk and meat protein in the same meal. Starches are also considered incompatible with milk and eggs.

Raw or Not?

One of the biggest controversies swirling around in the dog world is whether dogs should be fed a raw diet. After all, wolves don't cook their food. They don't know how. Still, dogs and wolves, while virtually identical genetically are often physically and certainly culturally very different. Raw foods are more difficult to digest and stay in the stomach longer. Combining raw and cooked foods is also not recommended; it is too hard on the Agni, the digestive fire. Before you decide on a raw food diet, consider the following points carefully.

- The safety of the meat supply is a worry. There is growing concern about meat inspection and contamination. Raw meat contains harmful pathogens, most of which are destroyed by proper cooking. Wild animals are often plagued by dangerous parasites often found in raw meats.
- The dog's palate. Studies show that dogs actually prefer cooked to raw meat.
- A wolf may eat a natural diet, but then wolves don't live a very long life, either.

That doesn't mean you should automatically start giving your dog dry kibble. In fact, dry food is not your best choice. In Ayurvedic terms, dry dog food provokes Vata (because of its dry, hard, rough texture) and Pitta (because of its additives, which can lead to aggression).

In the wild wolves eat raw meat. They not only eat it, but they stalk and kill their prey. The raw food they eat helps fuel their desire for stalking and killing. Domestic dogs don't live this lifestyle. Ayurvedic practitioners know that food has emotional as well as physiological effects. The live-prey diet is appropriate for wolves. It is not appropriate for most domestic dogs, who are better off having their food cooked and prepared for them. Vata dogs are especially unsuited to raw foods!

Grains

While dogs don't really require grains in their diet, most foods contain them. Here are the qualities of grains:

Sweet, astringent and cooling: barley, basmati rice, cereal, wheat bran, white rice.
Sweet, astringent, and warming: brown rice, corn and cornmeal, oats and oat bran.

Oils

Oils are often added to dog foods to provide essential fatty acids and to improve the skin.
Sweet, warming: Almond oil *(badam),* apricot oil, corn oil, safflower oil and mixed vegetable oil. Safflower and walnut oils have a secondary astringent taste. Sesame oil has a secondary bitter and astringent taste. Safflower is the best oil for Kapha dogs. It also helps dogs with heart and circulation problems. Almond oil is an excellent addition for dogs who have respiratory or kidney problems. It is said to build immunity and ojas. Corn oil nourishes the skin exceptionally well. Sesame oil is often considered the best of all oils. It lowers Vata and raises Pitta and Kapha and is an excellent tonic for all body tissues.
Sweet, cooling: Canola oil, sunflower oil.
Pungent, warming: Olive oil. Olive oil is good for dogs with liver problems. It is also good for the skin.
Sweet/Sour, warming: Flaxseed oil. Flaxseed oil is good for dogs with cough, as it draws mucus from the system.

Dairy

While many dogs can't tolerate some dairy products well, others – especially Vata dogs – usually can.
Sweet, cooling: cow's milk, ghee. Goat's milk has a secondary pungent taste, and butter a secondary astringent taste, and unsalted cheese a secondary sour taste.
Sour/Astringent, warming: Buttermilk, sour cream, and yogurt. Salted cheese has a secondary pungent taste.

Vegetables

Sweet/astringent, cooling: Broccoli, green beans, squash, sweet potatoes
Bitter/astringent, cooling: Bean sprouts, dandelion greens
Sweet/pungent, heating: Beets and beet greens, turnip greens.

Beans, Legumes, Peas

Sweet/Astringent, cooling: Black beans, black-eyed peas, chick peas, lima beans, pinto beans
Sweet/astringent, warming: Kidney beans, lentils, navy beans.

Spices and Herbs

Pungent, warming: Allspice, ajwain, anise, basil, black pepper, caraway, ginger, marjoram, nutmeg, oregano, parsley, pippali, savory
Pungent/Sweet, warming: Cardamom, mace
Bitter/Astringent: Fenugreek seed
Pungent/Salty, warming: Most varieties of seaweed
Bitter/Pungent, cooling: Coriander, dill
Sweet, pungent, cooling: Fennel.

For all Dogs

Quality

Dogs need a variety of different protein sources from an early age. Feeding a monotonous mono-diet is not only unnatural, but can lead to the development of allergies.

Choose only the highest quality dog foods, or, if you have the time, cook your dog's food yourself. All natural, organic foods for dogs (as for people) are best. Where possible avoid heavily processed, canned, or frozen foods.

Water should be fresh and freely offered. Pure spring water is best.

Additives

Avoid feeding your dog foods that contain artificial preservatives, flavors, or colors. Foods that require flavor enhancers have something wrong with them. And dogs don't care what color their food is.

Feeding Frequency

Feed your dog twice a day. If you must feed once a day, noon is the best time, when the digestive fires, or Agni are the strongest. Do not free feed. Free feeding leads to weight gain.

Serving

Serve food at body temperature or slightly warmer. Warm foods are more easily digested, promote Vata, and reduce Kapha. Overcooked food, however, reduces prana or life force, especially if cooked with heavy oils. Raw foods are not considered sufficiently tissue building in Ayurveda thought.

Stir fry, broiled, boiled, steamed, and grilled are all satisfactory ways to cook your dog's food. Regular frying destroys the prana (life-force) of the food. Avoid microwaved foods; microwaving destroys the natural Agni of the food.

Feed fresh food, which is rich in prana. Leftovers, unless fresh from your own meals that day, should be avoided. They tend to be heavy and changed in character from when freshly offered.

Don't feed your dog late at night. Dogs susceptible to bloat (Vata types) tend to do so several hours after eating, and if you feed your dog late at night, the attack may come on while you are asleep and thus not paying attention. In addition, most bloat attacks seem to occur at night. If possible feed your dog his evening meal at about 4 pm.

Food to Avoid

Avocadoes, onions, grapes and raisins, chocolate, macadamia nuts, alcohol, and xylotil (an artificial sweetener found in chewing gum) are all of which are toxic in varying degrees to dogs and should be avoided. Ayurveda also strongly discourages the feeding of mushrooms and other fungi to anyone.

Many dogs should not eat dairy, wheat, corn, and soy products. See below for more details. Yogurt is an exception. It is much easier to digest than milk, and most dosha types tolerate it well. Where allowable, add two tablespoons to meals to aid digestion.

White rice is preferred as it is easier to digest.

Storing Food

If you must feed your dog kibble, store it in a dry, cool place away from sunlight and temperature fluctuations. Most food should be kept in its original packaging, or in a special air-tight container. Don't use a plastic garbage can, even a clean one. These containers are often made of plastics that produce offensive or dangerous vapors. If the food smells bad, throw it out. Never keep any dry food more than a month, even in sealed containers.

A staple of Ayurvedic cooking is ghee *– clarified butter. The ancient sages called it* rasayana *– a "healing food." It is an anti-oxidant. Since it is free of milk solids it does not spoil easily. It actually stays fresh for weeks at room temperature. To make ghee, use unsalted, organic butter. To make ghee, melt a pound of butter in a medium saucepan. When the butter boils reduce the heat and simmer the uncovered butter for 45 minutes. The butter will start to "snap" and the milk solids will settle to the bottom, leaving the liquid ghee at the top. Sieve out the ghee into a clean glass jar and keep.*

Spices

A little spice improves flavors and can help maintain health. India is the homeland of great spices, and even dogs enjoy a little spice judiciously added to the diet. Of course, spices also have a medicinal role (in which case they are always called herbs). As long as you don't overdo it, a little spice might be helpful to your dog, as long as you use the appropriate ones for his dosha.

Food Allergies

While food allergies in dogs are not so common as many people believe, they can occur. In general, dogs tend to be intolerant or allergic to foods which contain too much of their own dosha. Therefore, Kapha dogs tend to be allergic to Kapha type foods such as dairy products and wheat. Pitta dogs tend to be intolerant to anything but bland foods. Vata dogs have problems with raw food, especially raw meats. They are also likely to be allergic to certain meat proteins.

You can test your dog for food allergies by omitting the suspect item or items (one at a time) from the diet. A protein is usually at fault – with beef as a primary suspect for many dogs. Corn, soybeans, and wheat can also cause allergies in many people and animals. Check below for foods to avoid for each dosha.

Feeding Seasonally

Serving foods in season is considered ideal. It is generally suggested that Pitta food should be avoided in summer, Vata foods in winter, and Kapha foods when it is damp or wet. Feeding food opposite to the season or weather is balancing. Just as we naturally eat warm spicy food in winter, and cool, bland foods in summer, so our dogs benefit from the same care. Remember that our domestic dogs have no choice in what they eat!

Feeding According to Dosha Type

Following are some general recommendations for feeding your healthy dog according to his type. These are foods that will balance his natural dosha. However, if a Vata dog, gets a Kapha disease, a Kapha-lowering diet might be called for. In chapter 8, I give dietary suggests for certain disease conditions. Those suggestions should be followed, as they are designed to address the disease mentioned. The instructions below are for healthy dogs, and will help prevent illness.

Feeding the Vata Dog

The basic principle for feeding a Vata dog is to feed them non-Vata foods; otherwise their system tends to get unbalanced. Vata foods are dry and cold and light. Look for warm, heavy, oily (not grease-soaked, of course!) foods for your Vata, dog or if your dog is suffering from a Vata disease.

Beneficial Foods for Vata Dogs

The proper diet for Vata dogs would emphasize sweet, sour, and salty tastes, and avoid bitter, pungent and astringent tastes. The last three are "air" tastes and increase the chance for abdominal trouble (including bloat) in Vata dogs. They do best when their food is cooked and warmed, as cold, raw foods are difficult to digest. The following foods are considered "Vata pacifying":
Dairy products: Soft cheese, yogurt, ghee. Most Vata dogs can even consume milk with little problem.
Grains: Wheat, rice, crackers.
Meats: Beef, buffalo, chicken, duck, turkey (dark meat only), fish.
Vegetables: Cooked carrots, pumpkin, and sweet potatoes, green beans. Cook all vegetables for Vata dogs.
Dietary Oils: Ghee, olive, sesame.
Spices: Anything but caraway. Use only very small amounts.
Supplements: Bee pollen, amino acids, spirulina (blue green algae), vitamin C and B complex.
Other: Eggs. For a real treat, give a pancake now and then.

Foods to Avoid

Vata dogs should avoid the following foods, especially in the fall and early winter when Vata is running high:
Meats: Lamb, pork, rabbit, venison, turkey (white meat).
Grains: Yeasty bread, white flour, brown rice.
Vegetables: Beans, corn products (including popcorn), white potatoes.
Other: Soy products, yeasty bread.
Spices: Caraway. fenugreek, saffron, coriander, turmeric, and parsley should be given only in minute amounts.
Supplements: Brewer's yeast.
Other: White sugar, dry dog food, pasta, soy products.

Feeding the Pitta Dog

Pitta dogs do best with sweet, bitter, and astringent tastes. They should avoid sour, salty, and pungent foods, all of which contain "fire" and increase the Pitta's chance of contracting a Pitta disease. Pitta-increasing foods are light, sharp, liquid and sour or pungent. To decrease Pitta in your Pitta dog, or if your dog has a Pitta condition, feed foods that are cold, heavy, and oily.

Beneficial Foods for Pitta Dogs

Pitta dogs thrive best on bitter, astringent, and sweet tastes.
Meats: Buffalo, chicken (white meat) and turkey (white meat), freshwater fish, shrimp, venison, rabbit.
Vegetables: Carrots, broccoli, sweet and white potatoes. Most sweet and bitter vegetables are allowable.
Dairy products: Ricotta cheese
Dietary oils: Canola, flaxseed, ghee, olive, primrose, sunflower, walnut
Spices: Basil, black pepper, caraway, cardamom, cinnamon, coriander, cumin, curry leaves, dill, fennel, fresh ginger, mint (peppermint, spearmint, wintergreen), neem leaves, orange peel, parsley, saffron, turmeric, tarragon, and vanilla in very small amounts.
Supplements: Brewer's yeast, spirulina (blue-green algae).
Other: Egg whites.

Foods to Avoid

Pitta dogs should avoid the following, especially in the late spring and summer, when Pitta is running high:
Dairy products: Yogurt and hard cheese.
Meats: Beef, chicken (dark meat) and turkey (dark meat), ocean fish, lamb, pork.
Vegetables: Most pungent vegetables.
Dietary oils: Corn, sesame, safflower, almond, apricot, sesame.
Spice: Ajwain, allspice, almond extract, anise, asafetida, basil (dried), bay leaf, cayenne, cloves, fenugreek, garlic, ginger, mace, marjoram, mustard, nutmeg, oregano, paprika, pippali, poppy seeds, rosemary, sage, salt, savory, star anise, thyme.
Supplements: Amino acids, bee pollen.
Other: Soy products, egg yolk, honey, molasses.

Feeding the Kapha Dog

Kapha dogs do best with pungent, bitter, and astringent tastes. Sweet, sour, and salty tastes tend to increase water, which is the last thing a Kapha dog needs. Kapha-increasing foods are cold, heavy, and oily. Look for foods with the opposite qualities for your Kapha dog's normal diet, or if you have a dog with a Kapha-related disease.

Kapha dogs do best with a weekly 24 hours fast to help them detoxify.

Foods Beneficial to Kapha Dogs

Kapha dogs do best on pungent, bitter, and astringent foods,
Dairy products: Goat's milk and ghee (in moderation).
Meat: Chicken and turkey (white meat), rabbit, venison,
Dietary Oils: Canola, almond, corn, ghee, or sunflower.
Vegetables: Carrots, white potatoes, green beans, broccoli. Most pungent and bitter vegetables are allowable.
Spices: All spices in small amounts are okay for Kapha dogs, but salt should be avoided when possible.
Supplements: Amino acids, bee pollen, brewer's yeast, spirulina (blue-green algae), vitamin C and B complex.
Other: Eggs.

Of all types, the Kapha dog has the most tolerance for dry food. Some even thrive on it.

Foods to Avoid

Most Kapha dogs should avoid overly sweet or salty foods, especially in the late winter and spring, when Kapha is high and Kapha dogs are most at risk.
Dairy products: Butter, yogurt, or cheese.
Meats: Beef, buffalo, chicken (dark) duck, ocean fish, lamb, pork.
Dietary Oils: Olive, safflower, primrose, or coconut.
Grains: Rice and rice cakes, wheat.
Vegetables: Sweet potatoes, kelp, pumpkin, squash, zucchini. Most sweet, juicy vegetables should be avoided.
Other: Soy products, fried foods, yeasty bread, white sugar, salt.

Chapter 5

Ayurvedic Herbs

While Ayurvedic medicine follows many paths, practitioners agree that herbal therapy is its most effective healing tool. The ancient Indian sage Charaka identified 350 medicinal herbs, divided into 50 groups. Part of the division depended upon whether the herbs in question had a healing or preventive effect. Of course, Charaka's herbs are native to the area in which he lived. Had he lived in Ohio, he would have found different ones, just as had he lived in Germany or France, he would have used German or French herbs. That being said, it is true that India does seem to possess an extraordinarily wide variety of medicinally effective herbs.

We cannot identify all 350 species with absolute certainty today and, of course, many other herbs, both Indian and Western, also have healing properties. In fact, about half of all pharmaceuticals presently sold are herbal in origin. Digitalis comes from the foxglove, pharmaceutical cortisone from yams, atropine from belladonna, reserpine from snakesroot (hear the "serpent" in the name), morphine from poppies, tubocurarine (a muscle relaxer from curare), and many antibiotics from fungi.

However, herbal remedies often differ from mainstream pharmaceuticals because herbalists use parts of the entire plant rather than the pharmaceutical practice of isolating specific active ingredients. Ayurvedic herbalists believe this results in a gentler, more natural cure in which the ingredients work together.

In this chapter, I am including a few of the Ayurvedic herbs. There is nothing especially magical about the Indian herbs traditionally used in Ayurvedic medicine. Some of them are also used as kitchen spices, and many of these have found their way into homes throughout the world. Others, whose use is primarily medical, seem more exotic, at least to westerners.

Many western plants have exactly the same Ayurvedic properties as do Indian herbs. However, the medical system we call Ayurveda was based upon Indian herbs, and it is only relatively recently that western Ayurvedic practitioners began looking for western herbal equivalents. This requires a careful study of each herb, to learn whether it is Vata-enhancing, Pitta-reducing, Kapha-balancing, and so on. Work in this area is ongoing.

However, here are some western herbs (or eastern herbs widely familiar to westerners) included in the traditional Ayurvedic *materia medica*. You can obtain many of these from your western herbal supplier, grocer, personal herb pot, or even from your backyard.

Here are few common kitchen herbs which Ayurvedic physicians use for their healing powers:

Barberry (Berberis vulgaris): Daruharidra
Basil (Ocimum sanctum): Tulsi
Black Pepper (Piper nigrum): Maricha
Cardamom (Elettaria cardamomum): Ela
Cinnamon (Cinnamomum cassia): Tvak
Castor oil (Ricinus communis): Eranda
Coriander or cilantro (Coriandrum sativum): Danyuk
Fenugreek (Trigonella foenum-graecum)
Lemongrass (Andropogon citrates): Bhutrin
Licorice (Glycerrhiza glabra)
Mint species (Mentha)
Red Raspberry: Gauriphal
Rhubarb (Rheum emodi and others): Amla vetasa
Sandalwood (Santalum album)
Sorrel (Oxalis corniculata): Changeri
Turmeric (Curcuma longa): Haridra
Violet (Viola odoarta): Trayman

The Name Game

Because an individual herb may have a multitude of common names, or the same common name may refer to more than one herb, when buying herbs, always check the scientific name, which is in two parts and the same all over the world. In this book, I am including the scientific name in parentheses after the common name I chose to use for each herb. I also include other names by which the herb is known, including in some cases, the Chinese herbal name. (India and China share some of the same botanicals.) There are hundreds more Ayurvedic herbs than I have listed here.

Preparing the Herbs

Even though modern medicines are largely derived from herbs, there are solid reasons for preferring whole herbs. Isolated ingredients, while powerful, often lack the balancing effect that is present in whole herbs. Whole herbs tend to work more slowly, but they are usually gentler and often have fewer side effects. However, for serious and emergency conditions, please do not attempt to medicate your dog yourself. See a knowledgeable holistic veterinarian.

For best results, you should visit an Ayurvedic healer with knowledge of dogs for healing prescriptions. Herbs are powerful medicine – that's one reason they work so well. Improperly prescribed or administered herbs can produce a multitude of deleterious side effects in your dog. This herb list is not intended to replace competent veterinary care.

You can also use many of these herbs as an aromatic oil.

In Ayurveda, herbs are generally not taken "raw, " but made into a tea or mixed into a vehicle such as water, milk, or honey. Since some of them have a bitter taste, this may be the only way you can persuade your dog to partake of them, anyway. It is always acceptable to mix herbs in some warm water or infuse them into a tea and serve with your dog's dinner. *In addition, nearly all these herbs are available in easy to use commercial preparations, usually accompanied by instructions.*

Because Ayurveda has a strong spiritual component, practitioners recognize the synergistic effect of reciting a "seed" mantra, or empowering sacred phrase, over the herbs before taking them. A seed mantra is known as a *bija*, and one of the most effective is this one:

Aum Ing Hring Shring
Kling Sanga Shamboah Namah

Don't go running to your Sanskrit dictionary! A seed mantra does not "mean" anything particular, although "*Aum*" is a universal word of tremendous mystery and force. The power is in the vibratory qualities of the sound. Repeat the seed mantra once, seven, or 108 times. The latter number has a mystical significance in Indian philosophy. Pause and listen between each repetition. I talk more about the power of sound in chapter 6.

The *taste cascade* refers to the series of energetic actions: the first taste *(rasa),* the cooling or heating effect *(virya),* and the final effect upon the body *(vipaka).*

Herb List

Ajwain *(Trachyspermum ammi* or *Carum ajowan* or *C. copiticum).* Known as omam in the southern part of India. English term: Bishop's weed.

- *Action:* Antispasmodic, anti-viral.
- *Ayurvedic Function:* Conquers Kapha and Vata.
- *Indications:* Heart problems, cough, digestive problems, including colic and flatulence. This is a favorite remedy to disperse wind in the bowels, and is used as a wormer. Mixed with buttermilk, it makes an antacid.
- *Parts Used:* Crushed seeds or fruit.
- *Preparation and/or Dosage:* A poultice of the crushed herb can be used for arthritis.
- *Taste Cascade:* Pungent/Warming/Pungent.
- *Note:* It is believed that the thymol is especially potent against coughs. This herb tastes like a cross between thyme and oregano and is often combined with ashwagandha, brahmi and guggul in heart formulations. This herb tastes something like thyme (but stronger) and is a relative of caraway/cumin.

Akarkara *(anacyclus pyrethrum).* Also called akarahahra and pellitory.

- *Action:* Stimulant, nerve tonic.
- *Ayurvedic Function:* Pungent and warming. It balances all doshas, but is pacifying to Vata and Kapha.
- *Indications:* Nerve disorders, tooth and gum disease, bowel problems.

- *Part Used:* Root.
- *Preparation and/or Dosage:* Powder, pills, or paste.
- *Taste Cascade:* Pungent/Warming/Pungent.

Aloe (*Aloe* spp.).

- *Action:* Antiseptic.
- *Ayurvedic Function:* Decreases Pitta.
- *Indications:* To heal minor wounds and burns, problems with the small intestine helps remove heavy metal, good for over-oily skin.
- *Parts Used:* Leaves, gel.
- *Preparation and/or Dosage:* Gel can be applied directly to wounds and burns. Powder may be used in VERY small doses.
- *Taste Cascade:* Sweet/Cooling/Sweet.
- *Note:* Do not use internally in pregnant animals.

Amla *(Emblica officinalis).* Also called amalaki or emblic myrobalan. English term: Indian gooseberry. Chinese herbal name: An Mwo Le.

- *Action:* The fresh fruit is cooling, diuretic and laxative. The unripe fruit is very acid. The dried fruit is sour and astringent. Flowers are cooling and aperient (gentle laxative). Bark is astringent. The herb is also hemostatic and a nutritive tonic. It is used to rebuild and maintain new tissues and increases red blood cell count. A naturally high source of Vitamin C (3,000 mg per fruit). Builds the immune system.
- *Ayurvedic Function:* Balance for Pitta.
- *Indications:* Heart, eye (cataracts) and nervous disorders, anemia, colitis, diabetes, fever. Many chronic conditions. All Pitta diseases. Amla is considered a potent antioxidant and a good astringent due mainly to its high content of polyphenols.
- *Parts Used:* Fruit (dried or fresh), nut or seed, leaves, root, bark, and flowers.
- *Preparation and/or Dosage:* Powder, decoction/infusion of leaves and seeds; essential oil; confection; powder; paste. Powder: 1/4 to 1/2 teaspoon. More will act as a laxative. Pill: 1/2 to 1 a day as required.
- *Taste Cascade:* Sour/Cooling/Sour.
- *Note:* No safety information available. The name of this herb means “nurse” and adequately reflects its function. This is

considered one of the best Pitta-cooling herbs. Amla is the main ingredient in an herbal honey formulation known as c *Chyawanprash,* the biggest selling Ayurvedic product in India.

Amla-vetasa *(Rheum emodi* and other species). Also called Aml Parni, revand-chini, archu. English term: Rhubarb.

- *Action:* Purgative, alterative, hemostatic, and antipyretic.
- *Ayurvedic Function:* Bitter, pungent, cooling. Reduces Pitta and Kapha; increases Vata.
- *Indications:* Protects the colon – can be used for both constipation and diarrhea. For older dogs add ginger or fennel.
- *Part Used:* Root (rhizome).
- *Preparation and/or Dosage:* Infusion, powder, pill. Use about 1/4 gram.
- *Taste Cascade:* Bitter/Cooling/Pungent.
- *Note:* Do not give to dogs with arthritis, epilepsy, or uric acid diseases. May cause diarrhea in Pitta dogs.

Arjuna *(Terminalia arjuna, Pentaptera glabra* or *augustifolia,* or *Arjuna Myrobalan).* Also called arjun, arjuna-sadra, attumarutu, billimatti, holematti, kahu, kukubha, maochettu, maruthu, nirmaruthu, rektarjuna, sadado, sajadan, sanmadat, shardul, tella-madoi, tormatti, vellai maruda-maram, vella-marda, and yermaddi.

- *Action:* Alterative, astringent, cardiotonic, hemostatic, rejuvenative, tonic and lithontriptic.
- *Ayurvedic Function:* Balances all doshas; excess may increase Vata.
- *Indications:* Heart problems (bark) and chronic urinary tract problems, bile. Wound healing (bark). Juice of leaves (ear problems).
- *Parts Used:* Bark or root.
- *Preparation and/or Dosage:* Decoction or powder (1 teaspoon). For fracture healing: Combine pulverized Arjuna bark with equal quantity of pulverized red sandalwood, sugar, and rice water. Pour over food.
- *Taste Cascade:* Astringent/Cooling/Pungent.
- *Note:* This is considered the best Ayurvedic herb for heart disease, but should not be used in dogs with heart arrhythmia.

Asafetida *(Ferula asafetida).* Also called hing, assafoetida, devil's dung, food of the gods.

- *Action:* Antispasmodic, nervine, stimulant to digestive and respiratory systems, digestive aid.
- *Ayurvedic Function:* It reduces Vata and Kapha and raises Pitta.
- *Indications:* Convulsions, flatulence, stomach pains, abdominal distention.
- *Parts Used:* Resin and gum. It is fried before using to make it less irritating.
- *Preparation and/or Dosage:* To make a tincture, put 2 oz. of the brown root gum powder in 6 oz. alcohol; let stand for 2 weeks and shake once daily. Strain and pour the liquid into an amber glass container. Use 5–10 drops in 6 fluid ounces for gastrointestinal distress.
- *Taste Cascade:* Pungent/Bitter/Bitter.
- *Note:* It has a horrible stench. Safety information not available. Some consider this the best therapeutic spice for Vata dogs.

Ashoka *(Saraca indica).* Also called anganapriya. Ashoka literally means "remover of sorrow." This is a medium sized evergreen found all over India.

- *Action:* Astringent, sedative, antidiarrheal.
- *Ayurvedic Function:* Decreases Vata.
- *Indications:* Promotes uterine health; this is its major use.
- *Part Used:* Bark.
- *Preparation and/or Dosage:* Decoction, powder, pill, paste.
- *Taste Cascade:* Astringent/Cooling/Pungen.
- *Note:* In warm regions, this plant can be cultivated for its lovely flowers. It is said that Buddha was born under an Ashoka tree.

Ashwagandha or ***Indian Ginseng*** *(Withania somnifera* or *Physalis flexuosa).* Also known as ashgandh, achuvagandi, amikkira-gadday, amkulang-kalang, amukkira-kilzhangu, amukran-kizhangu, asagandha, asana, asgandh, asundha, asvagandhi, fatarfoda, hirimaddina-gadday, hirre-gadday, penneroo-gadda, pevette, and sogade-beru English term: Indian ginseng, winter cherry.

- *Action:* Immune booster, mild sedative, tonic, alterative, astringent, nervine, anti-inflammatory, diuretic, anti-tumor, anti-stress (adaptogen), anti-oxidant. Ashwagandha stimulates the activation of immune system cells, such as lymphocytes. It has tissue-building properties and also gives energy and vitality.

- *Ayurvedic Function:* Reduces Vata and Kapha; increases Pitta. It is one of the best herbs for pacifying Vata in the fall.
- *Indications:* General debility, anemia (Vata and Kapha type), tumors, mental problems, immune deficiency, arthritis, inflammation, cancer, liver problems, exhaustion, arthritis (Vata and Kapha type), and weak eyes. It is a good geriatric tonic and is typically given to male rather than female dogs. The female equivalent is shatavari.
- *Parts Used:* Roots and leaves, dried.
- *Taste Cascade:* Bitter/Warming/Sweet.
- *Preparation and/or Dosage:* Decoctions, ghee, oil, powder (1/8–1 teaspoon). You can also give 500–1500 mg/day dried herb. Some Vaidyas prescribe 1 gram of the whole herb per day in capsule or tea form. To make a tea, boil the roots for 15 minutes and cool. Add to one cup of water once a day.
- *Note:* This herb belongs to the pepper family and is said that it possesses the combined effect of Siberian ginseng and echinacea. The name of this herb means "strong as horse!" and is actually supposed to smell like a horse. This is also a very "sattvic" herb and produces ojas in abundance. This is an Ayurvedic herb that is not used in traditional Chinese medicine. No significant side effects have been reported with this herb.

***Bacopa** (Bacopa Monniera).*

- *Action:* Nervine, diuretic, cardiotonic, brain tonic, sedative.
- *Ayurvedic Functions:* Lowers Vata and Kapha; raises Pitta.
- *Indications:* Asthma, joint pain, emotional stress. Helps mental acuity and memory.
- *Part Used:* Whole plant.
- *Preparation and/or Dosage:* 1 cup of infusion per day. Powder: 1 gram twice a day with water or food.
- *Taste Cascade:* Bitter/Cooling/Pungent.
- *Note:* This herb has similar powers to Brahmi, and is sometimes called Brahmi, although it is a different species. Bacopa is more potent.

Bala *(Sida cordifola).* Also called bariar, batyalaka, beejband, bijband, brela, chikana, chiribenda, chitimutti, hettuti-gida, janglimethi, kharenti, khareti, kisangi, kungyi, mayir-manikham, muttuva, paniyar-tutti, simak, tupkaria, tutturabenda, and velluram. English term: country mallow. The word "bala" means "strength-giving."

- *Action:* Analgesic, demulcent, diuretic, nervine, rejuvenative, stimulant, tonic, vulnerary. Removes toxins and builds immunity. Cardiac stimulant. This is one of the most frequently used Ayurvedic herbs, because it simultaneously balances all three doshas.
- *Ayurvedic Function:* Strengthens Pitta, balances Kapha. Pacifies Vata in the fall.
- *Indications:* For inner strength, urinary problems, nervous disorders, asthma, bronchitis, kennel cough, heart disease.
- *Parts Used:* Seeds, roots, leaves, stems.
- *Preparation and/or Dosage:* Decoction/infusion, powder, medicated oil. Generally, roots are given in infusion for nervous and urinary diseases, as well as for wound healing. Leaves can be applied to the eyes for ophthalmia. Roots, seeds, and leaves are used together as a cardiac toner.
- *Taste Cascade:* Sweet/Cooling/Sweet.
- *Note:* While this herb has been safely used in Indian medicine for many hundreds of years, do not attempt to medicate using this herb without guidance from a qualified practitioner. It is placed here for your information only, as it is so widely used. Bala is not used in traditional Chinese medicine.

Bhringaraj *(Eclipta alba).* Also called Kesharaja. Chinese herbal name: Han Lian. The name means "ruler of hair"! (When you see the word "raj" is means "ruler.")

- *Action:* Alterative, hepatic deobstruent, hemostatic, and antipyretic; the roots and leaves are cholagogues; the root is tonic, alterative, emetic, and purgative.
- *Ayurvedic Function.* Rejuvenates Pitta, but balances all doshas.
- *Indications:* Kidney and liver problems (viral hepatitis, hepatic enlargement). Good for the skin and coat, especially helpful in growing hair. Externally, a paste can draw out toxins and reduce inflammation.

- *Parts Used:* Herbs, roots, leaves.
- *Preparation and/or Dosage:* Infusion, decoction, powder, medicated oil. The root powder is used for hepatitis. Powder: Give 1 1/2 – 3 1/2 grams per day.
- *Taste Cascade:* Sweet/Cooling/Sweet, according to some authorities; Pungent/Warming/Pungent according to others.
- *Note:* Can cause chills.

Bhutrin *(Andropogon citrates).* Also called gandhatrana, harichha, aginghas, bhustrina. English term: Lemongrass.

- *Action:* Antispasmodic, diaphoretic, diuretic, emmenagogue, stimulant.
- *Ayurvedic Function:* Lowers Pitta and Kapha; raises Vata.
- *Indications:* Bowel spasm, diarrhea, fever, gas.
- *Parts Used:* Leaves and essential oil.
- *Preparation and/or Dosage:* Infusion of the leaves (1 in 5) or decoction of leaves (4 ounces of the grass to 1 pint of boiling water). Also use oil or powder.
- *Taste Cascade:* Bitter/Cooling/Pungent.
- This herb grows wild in India and Sri Lanka. Store lemongrass away from other herbs, as it may pick up other flavors.

Bitibaki *(Terminalia Belerica).* Also called bibhitaki, bhaira, or beleric myrobalan.

- *Action:* Laxative. Anthelmintic, antiseptic, astringent, lithotriptic.
- *Ayurvedic Function:* Balances Kapha and Pitta; increases Vata.
- *Indications:* Vomiting, coughing, chronic diarrhea, eye problems, Kapha digestive disorders.
- *Part Used: Fruit.*
- *Preparation and/or Dosage:* Infusion, decoction, powder, paste.
- *Taste Cascade:* Astringent/Warming/Sweet.
- *Note:* This herb is not used in traditional Chinese medicine. Do not use in cases of acute diarrhea.

Bilva or ***Bilwa*** *(Aegle marmelos).* Also called shivaphala. English term: Bael tree.

- *Action:* Astringent, digestive, stomachic (half ripe or unripe fruit). Laxative (ripe fruit).

- *Ayurvedic Function:* Reduces Vata and Pitta; increases Kapha.
- *Indications:* Bleeding, diarrhea, fever, vomiting.
- *Part Used:* Fruit.
- *Preparation and/or Dosage:* Use a little of the rind of the unripe fruit for diarrhea. The stem bark can be used for fever, and a leaf poultice for inflammations.
- *Taste Cascade:* Astringent/Cooling/Cooling.
- *Note:* This is one of the best herbs for chronic diarrhea.

Bitter Melon or ***Bitter Gourd*** *(Momordica charantia).* Also called karela, karavalla, kathilla (Sanskrit). English: also Balsam pear.

- *Action:* Helps regulate the body's ability to process sugars. Also antithelmic.
- *Ayurvedic function:* Reduces Pitta.
- *Indications:* For control of blood sugar levels. It has also been used to control scabies as an external application.
- *Parts Used:* Fruit and leaves.
- *Preparation and/or Dosage:* You can buy commercial capsules; give one twice a day with meal. For small dogs use half.
- *Taste Cascade:* Bitter/Cooling/Astringent/Bitter.
- *Note:* Bitter melon is also very rich in vitamins. The plant grows in both Asia and South America and contains gurmarin, a polypeptide similar to bovine insulin reported to have blood sugar regulating effects. The plant has at least three known compounds that lower blood sugar.

Bola *(Balsamodendron myrrha).*

- *Action:* Alterative, analgesic, antiseptic, antispasmodic, emmenagogue.
- *Ayurvedic Function:* Considered bitter. Astringent herb (despite the taste cascade). Reduces Vata and Kapha; increases Pitta in excess.
- *Indications:* Anemia, arthritis, kennel cough, injuries.
- *Part Used:* Resin.
- *Preparation and/or Dosage:* Infusion, powder, pill, paste.
- *Taste Cascade:* Sweet/Warming/Pungent.
- *Note:* In human Ayurvedic medicine, bola is considered to be an aphrodisiac. It has been valued since very ancient times for its detoxifying powers.

Brahmi *(Centella asiatica* or *Hydrocotyle asiatica).* Also called gotu kola, manduakaprni, and Brahma-manduki. Chinese herbal names: Chi-hsueh Ts'ao, man t'ien hsing, English term: Indian Pennywort.

- *Action:* Mild sedative, tonic, alterative, diuretic, febrifuge, nervine, rejuvenative. Supports memory. Blood cleanser, fever reducer. Produces calmness. Stimulates hair growth and mental activity.
- *Ayurvedic Function:* Balances all the doshas.
- *Indications:* Chronic venous insufficiency, skin ulcers, wound healing, minor burns, anxiety, Pitta type anemia, nervous disorders (including epilepsy), circulatory trouble, and age-related mental decline.
- *Part Used:* Whole plant.
- *Preparation and/or Dosage:* External: Applied as an oil for nervous disorders. Internal: Infusion, decoction, powder. The dried leaf can be made into a tea by a adding a teaspoonful to boiling water. And allowed to steep 15 minutes. Give one cup a day. Powder: Give 1/2 – 1 1/2 grams per day. Standardized extracts containing up to 100 per cent total saponins (triterpenoids), 30 mg once or twice per day can be given.
- *Taste* Cascade: Bitter/Cooling/Sweet.
- *Note:* This is considered the best herb for brain and nerve cells. It is the most sattvic of all herbs, producing mental clarity. The saponins in this plant may prevent excessive scar formation by inhibiting the production of collagen.

Brihati *(Solanum indicum).* Also called kantakari, birhatta. English: Indian sunplant, Indian Nightshade.

- *Action:* Astringent, carminative, cardiac tonic, resolvent. The root is diuretic, expectorant, and stimulant.
- *Ayurvedic Function:* Astringent.
- *Indications:* Kennel cough or dry coughs, fever, gas, edema, and enlarged spleen. This herb may have anti-tumor properties.
- *Parts Used:* Fruit, root, plant, seeds.
- *Preparation and/or Dosage:* Decoction, powder.
- *Taste Cascade:* Astringent/Astringent/Astringent.
- *Note:* This herb is found throughout India.

Changeri *(Oxalis corniculata).* Also called amrul, amlika. English term: Sorrel.

- *Action:* Cooling, astringent.
- *Ayurvedic Function:* Lowers Pitta and Kapha; raises Vata.
- *Indications:* Fever, inflammation, digestive problems. Traditionally used as a poultice or compress to remove warts.
- *Part Used:* Leaves.
- *Preparation and/or Dosage:* Juice, powder, paste, poultice, or pill.
- *Taste Cascade:* Astringent/Pungent/Cooling.
- *Note:* This herb is dangerous if overdosed. Use with care.

Chirayata *(Swertia chirata* or *Gentiana chirayita).* Also called bhunimba, bhuchiretta, charayatah, chiretta, chiraita, jwaranthakah, kirata, kiraita, kiriath, kiriyattu, kiryat, charayatah, mahatita, nila-vemu, nila-vembu, qasabuz-zarirah. English term: Indian gentian.

- *Action:* Bitter tonic, stomachic, febrifuge and anthelmintic, appetizer, laxative, alterative, antidiarrheic and antiperiodic.
- *Ayurvedic Function:* Reduces Pitta and Kapha. Increases *agni* (the digestive fire) and Vata.
- *Indications:* Good for fever, as well as heart, liver, and eye problems. This is a chief ingredient in many Pitta-type arthritis formulations.
- *Parts Used:* Leaves and whole plant.
- *Preparation and/or Dosage:* Infusion or powder; or 5 grains of the root with honey.
- *Taste Cascade:* Bitter/Bitter/Bitter.
- *Note:* Use of this herb may result in very high Vata. It is called the "King of the Bitters."

Chiretta *(Andrographis paniculata).* Also called kalmegh, kirata, kirata-tikta. Chinese herbal name: Chuan xin lian. English term: Andrographis.

- *Action:* Immune-stimulating, bitter tonic, antiseptic, anti-inflammatory, liver-protective, bile secretion-stimulating.
- *Ayurvedic Function:* Reduces Pitta and Kapha; increases Vata.
- *Indications:* Digestive problems, intermittent fevers, skin diseases, regulating the bowels.
- *Parts Used:* Roots (formerly), leaves and flowers.

- *Preparation and/or Dosage:* Capsules with dried herb or standardized extracts. For dried herb, 250–1500 mg twice a day. For standardized extract, 100 mg two times per day. For digestive problems, andrographis may be taken as a tea. Use 1 teaspoon (5 grams) of the herb for each cup of hot water. Allow the mixture to cool before giving.
- *Taste Cascade:* Bitter/Bitter/Bitter.
- *Note:* Good used in combination with antibiotics. The veterinary ointment Melicon V is prepared from this herb. The extract of the plant exhibits a significant anti-inflammatory activity.

Daruharidra *(Berberis vulgaris).* Also called daruhaldi. English term: Barberry.

- *Action:* Diuretic, antibilious, refrigerant, stomachic.
- *Ayurvedic Function:* Lowers Kapha and Pitta; raises Vata.
- *Indications:* Bile and urinary problems, Pitta detoxification.
- *Part Used:* Berries.
- *Preparation and/or Dosage:* Decoction, powder, eyewash, paste.
- *Taste Cascade:* Bitter/Astringent/Pungent.
- *Note:* This plants grows throughout the Himalayas, Nepal, Tibet, and Afghanistan, as well as Europe and the United States.

Dhanyak *(Coriandrum sativum).* Also call dhania. English term: Coriander/cilantro.

- *Action:* Alterative, antibilious, aromatic, carminative, diaphoretic.
- *Ayurvedic Function:* Balances all three doshas, but is especially good for Pitta disorders.
- *Indications:* Indigestion, vomiting, intestinal disorders, skin/rash problems, Pitta disorders.
- *Parts Used:* Seeds and Leaves.
- *Preparation and/or Dosage:* Infusions and powder.
- *Taste Cascade:* Bitter/Pungent/Cooling.
- *Note:* This is considered one of the main digestive herbs. Not indicated for extreme Vata types or animals with nerve tissue damage.

Ela *(Elettaria cardamomum).* Also called elachi. English term: Cardamom.

- *Action:* Carminative, diaphoretic, expectorant.
- *Ayurvedic Function:* Lowers Vata and Kapha; raises Pitta.
- *Indications:* Malabsorption, malnutrition, kennel cough, stomach, spleen, and pancreatic problems.
- *Part Used:* Seed.
- *Preparation and/or Dosage:* Infusion, powder.
- *Taste Cascade:* Sweet/Cooling/Pungent.
- *Note:* This is considered one of the main digestive herbs.

Eranda *(Ricinius communis).* Also called vatari or rendi. English term: Castor oil plant.

- *Action:* Cathartic, demulcent, analgesic, nervine.
- *Ayurvedic Function:* Pungent, sweet, hot. Raises all doshas.
- *Indications:* Abdominal disorders, itching. Castor oil is considered the "king of Vata disorders."
- *Part Used:* Oil.
- *Preparation and/or Dosage:* As a poultice for itching you can mix one part castor oil, 2 parts coconut oil, and six parts water.
- *Taste Cascade:* Sweet/Warming/Pungent.
- *Note*: This is an important herb for swellings and purging.

Fenugreek *(Trigonella foenum-graecum).* Also called uluhal.

- *Action:* Antiseptic, tonic, expectorant.
- *Ayurvedic Function:* Decreases Vata and Kapha but increases Pitta
- *Indications:* Diabetes mellitus, constipation, wounds, abscesses, arthritis, bronchitis.
- *Part Used:* Seeds.
- *Preparation and/or Dosage:* De-bitterized capsules, 3 grams per day.
- *Taste Cascade:* Pungent/Heating/Pungent.
- *Note*: Although not a native Indian plant, it has been used there for centuries. Do not use with pregnant dog. Fenugreek may interact with some medications; consult your holistic veterinarian. Its steroidal saponins (diosgenin, yamogenin, tigogenin, and neotigogenin) and mucilaginous fiber are thought to account for many of its beneficial effects. This herb should not be used in dogs with bleeding disorders.

Forskolli *(Coleus forskohli)*. Also called makandi, coleus.

- *Action:* Anti-spasmodic, smooth muscle relaxant, anti-coagulant, strengthens cardiac contractility, anti-allergic.
- *Indications:* Heart and lung disease, digestive ailments, flatulence, urinary tract infections, respiratory disorders, convulsions. Forskolin may help dilate blood vessels and improve the forcefulness with which the heart pumps blood. A preliminary trial found that forskolin reduced blood pressure and improved heart function in people with cardiomyopathy.
- *Parts Used:* Mostly root, occasionally the leaves.
- *Preparation and/or Dosage:* Cook roots in water and add to feed. Add cooked leaves to increase lactation. Coleus extracts standardized to 10–18 per cent forskolin are available. Give 25–5000 mg two to three times per day.
- *Taste Cascade:* Pungent/Warming/Pungent.
- *Note*. This is a mint. Very safe. Studies in healthy humanshave shown that direct application of an ophthalmic preparation of forskolin to the eyes lowers eye pressure. Do not apply the whole herb. Do not give to dogs with ulcers, as it may increase stomach acids. Certain drugs may interact with coleus. Discuss with your holistic veterinarian. The stems contain most of the active ingredient.

Frankincense or ***Shallaki*** *(Boswellia serrata)*. Known in India as salai guggul.

- *Action:* Anti-inflammatory, anti-arthritic, diuretic, demulcent, appetite stimulant, anti-fungal.
- *Ayurvedic Function:* Reduces Vata.
- *Indications:* Arthritis (especially of the knee), ulcerative colitis, chronic lung disease, diarrhea, allergies, liver disorders, ringworm and inflammatory skin conditions.
- *Parts used:* Bark and dried resinous gum.
- *Preparation and/or Dosage:* 75 mg of the pure boswellic acid three times a day; Today, extracts are typically standardized to contain 37.5–65 per cent boswellic acids which are anti-inflammatory.
- *Taste Cascade:* Pungent/Bitter/Warming.
- *Note*: Technically, only the resin and tree are called frankincense, but I like the name. Its use for arthritis has been scientifically documented; boswellic acids have a known anti-

inflammatory effect. As opposed to NSAIDs, long-term use of boswellia does not seem to cause irritation or ulceration of the stomach. Frankincense is particularly useful as an aromatic oil to pacify Vata dogs.

Gauriphal *(Rubus wallichi).* Also called red raspberry.

- *Action:* Alterative, antiemetic, astringent, hemostatic, tonic.
- *Ayurvedic Function:* Lowers Pitta and Kapha and increases Vata.
- *Indications:* Good for the female reproductive system during later pregnancy and delivery. Also good for diarrhea and Pitta disorders.
- *Part Used:* Leaves.
- *Preparation and/or Dosage:* Infusion, powder, paste.
- *Taste Cascade:* Sweet/Cooling/Sweet.

Ginger *(Zingiber officinale).*

- *Action:* Digestive tonic, cardiotonic.
- *Ayurvedic Function:* Lowers Vata.
- *Indications:* Motion sickness (both car and boat), osteoarthritis, abdominal bloating, coughing, vomiting, diarrhea.
- *Part Used:* Root.
- *Preparation and/or Dosage:* 250 mg of dried ginger powder can be taken one-half to one hour before travel, and then 250 mg every two to four hours as necessary.
- *Taste Cascade:* Pungent/Cooling/Warming.
- *Note*: Ginger may protect the stomach from the effects of NSAIDs such as Rimadyl. Certain drugs may interact with ginger. Talk to your holistic veterinarian. The dried rhizome contains 1–4 percent of volatile oils. These oils are also responsible for ginger's characteristic odor and taste. The aromatic constituents include zingiberene and bisabolene, while the pungent constituents are known as gingerols and shogaols. The pungent constituents are credited with the anti-nausea and anti-vomiting effects of ginger. Some ancient authorities recommend that fresh ginger be eaten daily; it is called the "universal medicine."

Guduchi *(Tinospora cordifolia).* Also called amrita, giloy. Chinese herbal name: Kuan Jin Teng.

- *Action:* Alterative, antiperiodic, bitter tonic. Inhibits bacterial growth, boosts the immune system.
- *Ayurvedic Function:* Bitter. Balances all doshas.
- *Indications:* Chronic diarrhea, bladder stones, allergies, arthritis, Pitta diseases. Debilitating ailments of all sorts.
- *Parts Used:* Fresh plant and juice, stem.
- *Preparation and/or Dosage:* Extract or powder. One capsule once a day before meals. Taken with Shilajit, it improves the immune system.
- *Taste Cascade:* Sweet/Hot/Sweet.
- *Note*: This herb is often used in combination with others in commercial formulations.

Guggul *(Comminphora mukul* or *Balsasmodendron mukul).* Also called gugulipid, gullula, mukul myrrh tree, gugul lipid, guggal. English term: Indian bedellium. Chinese Herbal Name: Mu Ku Er Mu Yao.

- *Action:* Demulcent, appetite stimulant, nervine, analgesic, antiseptic.
- *Ayurvedic Function:* Clears the blood channels. Reduces Kapha and Vata and increases Pitta.
- *Indications:* Arthritis, obesity, skin diseases, hypothyroid, low back pain, nervous disorders, weakness, bronchitis, digestive disturbances. An aid to fat metabolism. May enhance thyroid function. Indicated in disorders of lipid metabolism.
- *Part Used:* Gum resin from the stem.
- *Preparation and/or Dosage:* A common dose of guggulsterones is 10 mg three times per day. Most extracts contain 2.5–10 per cent guggulsterones.
- *Taste Cascade:* Salty/Hot/Pungent.
- *Note*: This plant is closely related to myrrh. This is the most important resin in Ayurvedic medicine. It is said to have purifying and rejuvenating powers. The raw resin is toxic and should not be used. Not to be used in dogs with liver or kidney disease, diarrhea, or inflammatory bowel disease. Not for long-term use. However, guggul as a single drug is rarely used in practice. One common commercial variety of guggul is called

Yograj Guggulu, sold primarily as an anti-arthritic herbal supplement.

Gymnema *(Gymnema sylvestra).* Also called gurmarbooti, gurmar, periploca of the woods, and meshasringi.

- *Action:* Astringent, diuretic, stomachic, tonic, hypoglycemic. Spleen and kidney tonic.
- *Ayurvedic Function:* Reduces Kapha and Vata; raises Pitta.
- *Indications:* Diabetes.
- *Parts Used:* Root and leaves.
- *Preparation and/or Dosage:* 1 to 2 grams per day divided into two doses. Give half an hour before a meal. Can be used with insulin, or in a few cases alone.
- *Taste Cascade:* Astringent/Warming/Pungent.
- *Note*: Contains gymnemic acids, which lower blood sugar. This herb has been used to treat diabetes for 2000 years. This is a safe herb, but it is not meant to be a replacement for insulin. Always consult your veterinarian if you suspect diabetes in your dog. Certain medicines may interact negatively with Gymnema.

Haridra *(Curcuma longa).* Also called haldi. English term: turmeric.

- *Action:* Alterative, anthelmintic, antibacterial, aromatic, carminative, stimulant. blood purifier.
- *Ayurvedic Function:* Lowers Kapha; raises Vata and Pitta.
- *Indications:* Anemia, arthritis, cough, diabetes, wounds, uveitis, liver problems.
- *Parts Used:* Rhizome and root.
- *Preparation and/or Dosage:* Infusion, decoction, powder, external paste with sandalwood. For uveitis: give 185 mg oral curcumin supplementation of turmeric extract with 95 per cent curcuminoids three times daily for 12 weeks for chronic anterior uveitis (inflammation of the iris and middle coat of the eyeball). For other conditions, turmeric extracts can be taken in the amount of 175–275 mg three times per day.
- *Taste Cascade:* Pungent/warming/pungent.
- *Note*: Do not use with pregnant dogs or strongly Pitta dogs. Otherwise it is very safe. There are no known drug interactions.

Haritaki *(Terminalia Chebula).* Also called harad, hardha. harh. English Term: myrobalan, Indian gall nut. Chinese herbal name: He Zi.

- *Action:* Rejuvenating, tonic, astringent, laxative.
- *Ayurvedic function:* Balances Vata.
- *Indications:* Liver problems, coughing, anemia, vomiting. Externally for Vata swellings.
- *Part Used:* Fruit.
- *Preparation and/or Dosage:* Decoction, powder, paste. Give 1/2 teaspoon of whole turmeric bid or 250 mg of cucumin.
- *Taste Cascade:* Salty/Warming/Sweet.
- *Note*: In Buddhist art, this plant is sometimes depicted in the extended palm of the Buddha. Balances Vata. This Tibetan "king of medicine," is a classic heart-brain-longevity tonic.

Jatamansi *(Nardostachys jatamansi).* Also called jatamanshi, jatamashi, balchar, achte narde, balacharea, balchir, bhut-jatt, bhytajata, duk, jaramanshi, jatamamshi, jatamanchi, jatamasi, jatamavshi, jatamavashi, jatamsi, jeta-manchi, kuki-lipot, narde indike, nard indien, sambul-u-'l hind, Sumbula- theeb, sunbuluttib, and tapaswini. English term: muskroot; Indian spikenard. Chinese herbal name: Chi Yi Gan Song Xiang.

- *Action:* Sedative (related to western herb valerian), aromatic, antispasmodic, carminative, deobstruent, digestive stimulant, diuretic, emmenagogue, nervine, reproductive, tonic.
- *Ayurvedic Function:* Balances all doshas.
- *Indications:* flatulence, bladder stones, allergies, epilepsy, skin conditions.
- *Parts Used:* Rhizome, rhizome oil.
- *Preparation and/or Dosage:* Infusion, powder.
- *Taste Cascade:* Astringent/cooling/pungent.

Note: Often used in combination with cinnamon and aloe.

Kustha *(Saussurea lappa).* Also called kut, kushtha. English term: costus.

- *Action:* Anthelmintic, antiseptic, astringent, antispasmodic, alterative.
- *Ayurvedic Function:* Pungent, bitter, warming. Balances all doshas.

- *Indications:* Coughing, bleeding.
- *Part Used:* Root.
- *Preparation and/or Dosage:* Powder, paste.
- *Taste Cascade:* Astringent/Astringent/Astringent.

Licorice *(Glycerrhiza glabra).* Also called yashtimadhu, mithi-lakdi, mulathi, liquorice, sweetwood, and licorice root.

- *Action:* anti-inflammatory, demulcent, anti-hepatotoxic, anti-spasmodic, emetic, expectorant, laxative, rejuvenative, sedative, and tonic. Calms the mind, harmonizes.
- *Indications:* Infection, liver and endocrine problems.
- *Part Used:* Dried peeled root.
- *Preparation and/or Dosage:* Decoction, milk decoction, powder, and ghee. Put 1/2 teaspoonful of the root in a cup of water, bring to a boil and simmer for 10–15 minutes, twice daily. Licorice root in capsules, 2.5–3 grams per day, can also be given. Certain medicines may interact with licorice. Contains glycyrrhizin, which has anti-inflammatory actions and may inhibit the breakdown of the cortisol produced by the body. Licorice flavonoids and the closely related chalcones, help heal digestive tract cells. They are also strong anti-oxidants which help protect liver cells.
- *Taste Cascade:* Sweet/Warming/Sweet.

Manjisthra *(Rubia cordifolia).* Also called manjit. English Term: Indian madder. Chinese herbal name: Qian Cao Gen.

- *Action:* Alterative, antitumor, astringent, diuteretic.
- Ayurvedic Functions: Lowers Pitta and Kapha; raises Vata.
- *Indications:* Fever, chronic urinary problems, chronic skin problems, wounds, edema, blood and Kapha disorders.
- *Parts Used:* Root.
- *Taste Cascade:* Sweet/Cooling/Pungent.
- *Note*: Manjisthra is considered to be the best all-round herbal blood purifier according to Ayurvedic literature.

Maricha *(Piper nigrum).* Also called gulmirch. English term: black pepper.

- *Action:* Stimulant, expectorant, carminative.
- *Ayurvedic Function:* Lowers Vata and Kapha; raises Pitta.

- *Indications:* Coughing, chronic indigestion, colon toxins, fevers.
- *Parts Used:* Dried unripe fruit.
- *Preparation and/or Dosage:* Infusion, powder.
- *Taste Cascade:* Pungent/Warming/Pungent.
- *Note*: In most circumstances, avoid giving Pitta dogs black pepper. It is considered excellent for "burning up" Ama.

Myrrh *(Commiphora molmol and C. myrrha).*

- *Action:* Cardiotonic, anti-arthritic, anti-inflammatory.
- *Ayurvedic Function:* Reduces Vata.
- *Indications:* Gingivitis, back pain, arthritis.
- *Part Used:* Resin from the stem.
- *Preparation and/or Dosage:* Dab the undiluted tincture in the mouth.In addition, tincture of myrrh, 1/2–1 teaspoon three times per day, can be given.
- *Taste Cascade:* Bitter/Pungent/Bitter.
- *Note*: No adverse effects of myrrh or drug interactions with myrrh have been reported. The three main constituents of myrrh are the resin, the gum, and the volatile oil. The resin has reportedly been shown to kill various microbes and to stimulate macrophages (a type of white blood cell).

Neem *(Azadirachta indica).* Also called nimba, nimmi, nimb, Indian lilac, bead tree, holy tree, margosa tree, nim, Persian lilac, Indian lilac, pride of China, ravipriya, veppu. Chinese herbal name: Lin Du Ku Lian.

- *Action:* Anthelmintic (tree bark, juice, and fruit), antiseptic, discutient (leaves), diuretic, anti-fungal, antiviral (leaves and tree bark), insecticidal tonic (root bark and oil from seed), astringent (tree and root bark), stimulant (flowers), tonic (flowers), stomachic (flowers), purgative (fruit).
- *Ayurvedic Function:* Reduces Pitta and Kapha. Increases Vata.
- *Indications:* Eye problems, allergies (oil in a sesame base), gastrointestinal upset, chronic low fever, skin diseases, Pitta-type anemia, ulcers, wounds, blood disorders, parasites, gum disease, arthritis, chronic fatigue.
- *Part Used:* Entire plant.
- *Preparation and/or Dosage:* Infusion, decoction, powder, medicated ghee, or oil. Neem is a wonderful tonic for spring and summer because of its cooling qualities. Not recommended

for Vata dogs, especially in the winter. 1–2 teaspoons of leaf juice or 1–2 grams of powdered leaf. Creams containing 5 per cent or more of neem oil or neem extracts are typically applied twice per day for skin infections.
- *Taste Cascade:* Astringent/cooling/pungent.
- *Note*: Neem has no known drug interactions. Its major constituents: terpenoids such as azadirachtin are considered to be antimicrobial and insect repellent among many other effects.

Pashana Bheda *(Saxigraga ligulata).* Also called pakanbed, dakachru.

- *Action:* Astringent, demulcent.
- *Ayurvedic Function:* Astringent. Lowers Pitta and Kapha; raises Vata.
- *Indications:* Helps dissolves uric acid and struvite bladder stones.
- *Part Used:* Rhizome.
- *Preparation and/or Dosage:* Decoction, powder, paste.
- *Taste Cascade:* Sweet/Cooling/Sweet.

Phyllanthus *(Phyllanthus amarus).* Also called bahupatra and bhuiamla.

- *Action:* Hepato-protective, astringent, stomachic, diuretic, febrifus.
- *Ayurvedic Function:* Reduces Kapha and Pitta; increases Vata.
- *Indications:* Hepatitis, pain, eye problems, constipation, gastric pain, edema, eczema.
- *Part Used:* Whole plant.
- *Preparation and/or Dosage:* Leaves and roots can be made into a poultice with rice water for edema and cutaneous ulcers; juice of the leaves for eye disorders. Internal: 300 mg per day of the powder.
- *Taste Cascade:* Astringent/Cooling/Cooling.
- *Note*: The roots have been used for centuries to help camels with digestive problems, so if you have a camel, you know what to use. No side effects or drug interactions have been reported with this herb.

Pippali *(Piper longum)*. Also called pipal. English term: long pepper. Chinese herbal name: Bi Ba.

- *Action:* Analgesic, carminative, expectorant.
- *Ayurvedic Function:* Pungent, sweet, warming. Lowers Vata and Kapha; raises Pitta.
- *Indications:* abdominal tumors and bloat, Kapha disorders.
- *Part Used:* Fruit.
- *Preparation and/or Dosage:* Infusion, powder, oil.
- *Taste Cascade:* Pungent/Hot/Sweet.

Punarnava *(Boerhavia diffusa)*. Also called vakhakhaparo, dholia-saturdo, tambadivasu, ghetuli, mukaratee-kirei, punernava, raktakunda, shothaghni, varshabhu, and kommegida. English term: spreading hogweed, horse purselane.

- *Action:* Longevity enhancer. Seeds are tonic, expectorant, carminative.
- *Ayurvedic Function:* Decreases Vata and Kapha. Increases the functioning of six of the seven bodily tissues (plasma, blood, muscle, fat, bone marrow and nerves, and reproductive tissue). Astringent to the bowels.
- *Indications:* Kidney problems and bladder stones, Kapha-type anemia.
- *Parts Used:* Whole herb, leaves, seeds, root.
- *Preparation and/or Dosage:* Juice, decoction, infusion, powder, paste.
- *Taste Cascade:* Bitter/Cooling/Pungent.
- *Note*: This herb is not used in Chinese herbal medicine. In color therapy, this herb can be used for "red."

Sandalwood *(Santalum album)*. Also known as chandana, white sandalwood, white saunders, yellow sandalwood. In India: chandan, chandanam, safed ghandan, srigandha.

- *Action:* alterative, antibacterial, antiseptic, astringent, carminative, disinfectant, diuretic, expectorant, hemostatic, refrigerant, sedative, stimulant.
- *Ayurvedic Function:* Reduces Pitta.
- *Indications:* Skin disease (including allergies), eye disease, infections of the urinary tract.
- *Parts Used:* Wood and volatile oil.

- *Preparation and/or Dosage:* Hot or cold infusion; decoction, powder (250 mg), medicated oil. To make a decoction: boil 1 teaspoon sandalwood in a cup water. Give a cup per day. For skin problems: make a tincture by dissolving 20 sandalwood drops in water and apply to the infected area. Alternately, use the diluted oil directly on the skin.
- *Taste Cascade:* Astringent/Cooling/Cooling.
- *Note*: A few dogs have an irritated skin response to sandalwood. Do not use in dogs with lung congestion.

Shatavari (Various species: *Asparagus racemosus, A. sarmentosus, A. gonoclados,* or *A. adscendens).* Also called shatamuli, chatavari, satavar. English term: hundred-husbands, wild asparagus. Chinese Herbal name: Tian men dong.

- *Action:* Antidiarrhetic, antispasmodic, aphrodisiac, anti-dysenteric, demulcent, diuretic, galactagogue, nutritive, mucilaginous, refrigerant, stomachic, tonic.
- *Ayurvedic function:* Blood cleanser, nourished mucous membranes. Increases Kapha, decreases Pitta and Vata. It is particularly useful for balancing Pitta.
- *Indications:* Skin problems (including allergies), cancer, Pitta type anemia, general debility, diarrhea, spastic colon, stiff joints. Female reproductive problems. Boosts the immune system.
- *Part Used:* Root.
- *Preparation and/or Dosage:* Decoction, powder, ghee, oil. 1 1/2 – 3 grams a day with honey. Or one capsule a day.
- *Taste Cascade:* Bitter/cooling/sweet.
- *Note*: Don't use with congested dogs. This herb works better with female dogs, and is the female "equivalent" of ashwagandha.

Shilajit. Also called mineral pitch.

- *Action:* Alterative, diuretic, lithiotriptic, antiseptic.
- *Ayurvedic Function:* Bitter, pungent, heating (its smell is sometimes compared to the smell of stale cow's urine.) It balances all doshas, but can be dangerous in strongly Pitta dogs.
- *Indications:* This is a tridoshic immune boosting substance.
- *Part Used:* Mineral – asphalt.

- *Preparation and/or Dosage:* As a powder with milk: 1/4 teaspoon twice a day.
- *Taste Cascade:* Pungent/Bitter/Warming.
- *Note:* This is not an herb, but is sometimes included in herbal formulations. It is composed of vegetable organic matter. However, in the Charaka *Samhita*, Shilajit is described as a product of four minerals: gold, silver, copper and iron. The Susruta *Samhita* adds lead and zinc.

***Trayman** (Viola odorate).* Also called vanpsa, banaphsa. English term: wild violet.

- *Action:* Emetic; demulcent, diaphoretic (flowers).
- *Ayurvedic Function:* Bitter, cooling. Balances all three doshas.
- *Indications:* Cough, respiratory problems.
- *Parts Used:* Flowers, root.
- *Preparation and/or Dosage:* Decoction, infusion, powder, pill.
- *Taste Cascade:* Bitter/Cooling/Bitter.

Tulsi or ***Holy Basil*** *(Ocimum sanctum).* Also called tulasi, krishnamul, and kala tulasi. English term: basil, common basil, sweet basil, St. Josephwort.

- *Action:* Antioxidant, demulcent, antispasmodic, appetizer, carminative, galactagogue, stomachic. Fights stress, relieves depression, and balances the mind.
- *Ayurvedic Function:* Maintains the digestive fire (agni). Lowers Vata and Kapha; raises Pitta.
- *Indications:* Diabetes, bronchitis, stomach cramps, coughs/flu, difficult urination, vomiting, constipation, and enteritis, as well as for general ailments of the throat, chest, and lungs. Tulsi leaves are specific for many fevers.
- *Parts Used:* Leaf, seeds, root.
- *Preparation and/or Dosage:* Infusion, powder, or in ghee. Steep 1/2 teaspoon of dried herb in 1/4 cup water. Take once a day. Can be sweetened with honey for palatability. Infusion (1 – 1 1/2 ounces).
- *Taste Cascade:* Pungent/Warming/Pungent.
- *Note*: Approved in Canada as an over-the-counter drug. Don't use for fevers or active infections.

Tvak *(Cinnamomum cassia).* Also called dalchini, daruchini. English term: Cinnamon.

- *Action:* Alterative, analgesic, antibacterial, antifungal, antiseptic, anti-arthritic, antispasmodic, aromatic.
- *Ayurvedic Function:* Lowers Vata and Kapha; raises Pitta.
- *Indications:* Weakness, liver problems, heart problems.
- *Part Used:* Bark.
- *Preparation and/or Dosage:* Infusion, decoction.
- *Taste Cascade:* Astringent/Hot/Pungent.

Vacha *(Acorus calamus).* Also called Bach. English term: calamus, sweet flag. Chinese herbal name: Chui chang.

- *Action:* Antispasmodic, decongestant, nervine, emetic, expectorant.
- *Ayurvedic Function:* Lowers Vata and Kapha; raises Pitta.
- *Indications:* Arthritis, coughing, rejuvenation.
- *Part Used:* Rhizome.
- *Preparation and/or Dosage:* Decoction, powder, paste. 1/2 teaspoon boiled 4–5 minutes in 1 1/2 cups water) milk decoction with powdered ginger (for digestive indications).
- *Taste Cascade:* Astringent or bitter/warming/pungent.
- *Note*: Although this herb has been used in Ayurvedic medicine for centuries, the FDA presently classifies sweet flag as an unsafe herb for internal usage.

Vasaka *(Adhaoda vasika).* Also called adosa. English term: Malabar nut.

- *Action:* Expectorant, diuretic, antispasmodic.
- *Ayurvedic Function:* Bitter, astringent, pungent, cooling. Lowers Pitta and Kapha; raises Vata.
- *Indications:* respiratory problems.
- *Parts Used:* Leaves, roots, flowers, bark.
- Dosage and Preparation: Infusion, extract, decoction.
- *Taste Cascade:* Bitter/Astringent/Cooling.
- *Note*: This is the main respiratory herb.

Vidari *(Ipomoea digitata, Ipomoea paniculata, Ipomoea mauritiana).* Also known as vidari-kanda, bilai-kand, palmudukan kizhangu, bhumikusmanda, balaikand. English term: Kudzu root. Chinese herbal name: Ge Gen.

- *Action:* alterative, aphrodisiac, cholagogue, demulcent, diuretic, emmenagogue, galactogogue, mucilaginous, rejuvenative, tonic.
- *Ayurvedic Function:* Pacifies Vata in the fall.
- *Indications:* Liver, spleen, and digestive problems.
- *Part Used:* Tuberous root.
- *Preparation and/or Dosage:* Powder, confection, decoction, milk decoction.
- *Taste Cascade:* Sweet/Cooling/Sweet.
- *Note*: Safety information on this herb not available.

Common Dosha-Altering Kitchen Herbs

Some Herbs to Increase Pitta

Anise, asafetida, bay leaves, black pepper, caraway, cayenne, cardamom, cloves,fenugreek, horseradish, marjoram, black pepper, oregano, poppy seeds, rosemary, sage, shatavari, thyme.

Some Herbs to Decrease Pitta

Chamomile, cinnamon, manjishtha, turmeric, kajuka, yellow dock, bhringaraj.

Some Herbs to Increase Vata

Caraway/cumin, chamomile, cloves, horseradish, oregano,

Some Herbs to Decrease Vata

Anise, asafetida, bay leaves, black pepper, cayenne, fenugreek, mustard, rosemary.

Some Herbs to Increase Kapha

Horseradish, marjoram, oregano, poppy seeds.

Some Herbs to Decrease Kapha

Anise, asafetida, bay leaves, black pepper, caraway/cumin, cayenne, cloves, fenugreek, mustard, rosemary, thyme.

Some Tridosha Balancing Herbs

Cumin, dill, fennel, nutmeg, peppermint, spearmint.

Traditional Herbal Combinations

Many Ayurvedic practitioners recommend using herbs in combination, as single herbs may over time produce unbalancing effects. If properly prepared, they are believed to have added effectiveness . Many of these are available commercially.

Triphala (Three Fruits)

This classic (it is described in the *Charaka*) Ayurvedic remedy is made from equal parts of the fruit of three trees: Amla (also called amalaki) or *(E. officinalis),* Baheda or bibbitaki *(T. belerica),* and Harada or haritaki *(T. chebula).* Each of the three constituent herbs balances one of the doshas: Amla balances Pitta, Harada balances Vata, and Bibbitaki balances Kapha. Therefore all three doshas are balanced. It builds Ojas (inner strength). It is usually given by adding 1/2 teaspoon of the powder to boiling water; steep for ten minutes and cool. It has a bitter taste so mix it well into the dog's food. It is excellent for allergies.

For the Older Dog: Rejuvenating Herbal Mixes:

Vata Dogs: *Ashagandha* – 1/2 teaspoon in warm milk twice a day.
Pitta dogs: *Shatavari* – 1/2 teaspoon in room temperature milk twice a day
Kapha dogs: *Punarnava* – 1/2 teaspoon twice a day in warm water or chicken broth

Dashamoola (a combination of ten herbs) is often prescribed for anemia in Vata dogs (especially in the fall).

Digestive Fire: A mixture of ginger, black pepper and pippali. Used to support metabolism, burn fat, and destroy toxins.

Kaishore Guggulu: Pacifies Pitta inflammation in joints. Also indicated for anemia.

Triphala: is used for detoxificiaton and cleansing. It is a balancing herbal combination, and works best when taken over a long period of time. It is good for all doshas.

Trikatu: A formulation of black pepper, ginger and pippali. It is used as a digestive aid and to clear Ama and excess Kapha from the system.

Quick Picks!

(I have included some western herbs on this list as well.)

Alteratives: aloe, sandalwood, black pepper, cinnamon, myrrh, and safflower.
Antacid: marshmallow root and leaf, meadowsweet herb, hops flower, and vacha.
Antibiotic: turmeric and echinacea.
Antidiarrheal: anantmula, lodhra, manjishtha, blackberry, comfrey, gentian, red raspberry, yellow dock, black pepper, ginger.
Antiemetic: pomegranate, licorice, amla, ginger, cloves, coriander, and raspberry.
Antiperiodic: Barberry, chirayata, guduchi, kutaj, and vacha.
Antiseptic: aloe, chitrak, gokshura, gudmar, sandalwood, and turmeric.
Antispasmodic: ginger, fennel, gokshur, pippali, camomile, ashwagandha, basil, guggul, licorice, bramhi, jatamanshi, peppermint, sandalwood, and spearmint.
Bladder or Kidney Stones: castor oil, kutki, pashanabheda (Bergenia ligulata), nishottar, chitrak.
Bleeding: lodhra, ashok, turmeric, licorice, durba, goldenseal, red raspberry, cinnamon, ginger.
Blood Cleanser: Equal parts of manjusthra and neem.
Body Ache: gokshura, ajwan, vala, licorice
Brain Disorders: Bacopa.
Cholagogue: Arka, guduchi, licorice, safflower, senna, and sesame.
Cleansing Tonic: Tinospora.
Cooling Herbs: Aloe, neem, manishtha, sandalwood, red clover, burdock.
Cough Relief: Pippali, dhamasa.
Diabetes: amalaki, blackberry, fenugreek, gudmar, senna, and shilajit.
Digestive Aid (stimulates Agni): asafetida, chitrak, ginger, trikatu, ajwan, hinga, pippali, black pepper.
Diuretic: Parsley, apamarga, ashwagandha, barberry, cardamom, cinnamon, ginger, gotu kola, gokshura, gudachi, licorice, and sandalwood.
Epilepsy: brahmi.
Expectorant: ginger, licorice, calamus, cardamom, cinnamon, cloves, sage, eucalyptus, thyme.

Fever Reducers: anantamul, patha, ginger, kiraita, Triphala, amalaki, black pepper, brihati, nirgundi, safflower, sandalwood.
Flatulence and Gas Reliever: bibhitaki, coriander, fennel, peppermint, ajwan, basil, cardamom, cinnamon, ginger, turmeric.
Heart Tonic: pomegranate, mango, raisins, arjuna, punarnava, guduchi, gokshura.
Inflammation Reducing: cumin.
Itch Relief: sandalwood, karanja, neem, turmeric.
Laxative: castor oil, flax seed, psyllium, rhubarb, senna.
Mood Altering: ashawaganda.
Pain Relief: guggul, rasna, ginger, shirish, myrrh, ashok, jatamansi, camphor, chamomile, cinnamon, cloves, echinacea, lavender flower, feverfew.
Sedative: ashwagandha.
Strength Promoting: bala, ashwagandha, shatavari.
Swelling Reduction: punarnava, ginger, gokshur, bibhitaki.
Tissue Building: bibhitaki, shatavari, ashwagandha, vidari.
Tonic (General): Aloe, bala, barberry, chirayata, guduchi, katuka, gentian, goldenseal.
Vitality Enhancer: amla, licorice, punarnava, guduchi, brahmi, vacha, haritaki.
Warming Herbs: ajwan, bayberry, black pepper, cayenne, cinnamon, ginger, haritaki, myrrh, safflower.
Weakness: amla.
Wound Healing: arjun, gulwel, licorice, lodhra

Chapter 6

Sense Therapy: Light, Fragrance, Sound and Touch

Dogs and people have a great deal more in common than in differences. Both species rely on five senses: sight, hearing, touch, smell, and taste, although dogs rely more on scent and less on eyesight than people do. Each sense has its place in Ayurvedic medicine. We covered the six tastes and their effects in chapter 4. Now we will talk about the more subtle senses.

Light Therapy: Crystals and Colors

Crystals and Metals

The power of various crystals and metals to promote healing is an integral part of many cultures and India is no exception. In modern times, there is a renewed interest in the vibrational qualities of crystals especially.

Gems

Healing stones are clear and devoid of flaws. In Ayurvedic theory, they serve as agents of electromagnetic energy, especially when they are embedded in pure metal like copper, silver, or gold. Wearing gems as ornaments or tucking them into bedding releases their energy. In traditional Ayurvedic therapy, the major gems were associated with planets, which were believed to produce negative energy. The positive energy of the gem cancelled out the negative energy from the planets.

Cracks, cloudiness, opaqueness, and inclusions may lower the effectiveness of the stone. In any case, you will not need to deck

Gems also tend to absorb the qualities of their previous owners, so if you are buying a stone it should be purified before placing in on your dog's collar or in his bedding. Don't simply use one of your own gems without first doing this! Placing the stone in cow's milk or salt-water overnight is the traditional method of purifying a stone.

your dog out in thousands of dollars worth of jewelry for him to get the beneficial effects of crystals. Their main purpose in Ayurveda is healing, not ornament. In addition, crystals are an *adjunct therapy* not intended to be replaced by competent veterinary care.

Healing crystals absorb and radiate light energy, which is manifested as color, including color beyond the range of human or canine vision. It does not matter that dogs are not good at distinguishing most colors. (Human beings can't detect x-rays, either, but that doesn't mean they have no effect.) The different colors (vibrations) have different effects on different parts of the body. No two gem species are precisely the same color or have the same vibrations. They may be *close*, but they are not exactly the same.

Color therefore becomes an important element in the healing power of crystal. In all cases, the larger the stone, the better. Most Ayurvedic gemstones are a minimum of two carats, with five carats being preferred. However, a large stone with flaws is less effective than a smaller, more perfect one.

Your dog can benefit from the healing powers of crystal in several ways. You can attach the crystal to his collar ring or even place one under his bed. Much gem-lore is laced with ancient folk wisdom. However, we are learning more and more every day about the power of vibrational and color therapy.

Sometimes gems are not just worn, but prepared as gem tinctures. The gems are soaked in a 50–100 per cent alcohol solution. Hard gems are soaked from one full moon to the next. Softer stones are soaked for a shorter time or in weaker solutions. They can then be ground into a paste and fed with a little pepper or honey, although this is not the best use for gems.

In India, Ayurvedic preparations exist in which gems are burnt into ash (*bhasma*). Traditionally, gems were crushed or burnt in long processes to make the ash, then fed either alone or with herbs. Some Ayurvedic practitioners believe their use in this way is more effective and works more quickly than with herbs. However, the expense is prohibitive, and there is no evidence that this claim is even true.

Rubies and Sapphires are identical in chemical structure. Their differing colors are result of different additives, such as chromium for rubies (the same element that makes emeralds green). The mineralogical term for both rubies and sapphires is corundum. Red corundum is called ruby, all other varieties are called sapphires. The same is true of emeralds, which are really a form of beryl. Of all the many varieties of beryls, including aquamarine, the grass-green variety is called emerald.

Most precious stones come in synthetic versions. These have precisely the same chemical composition as natural stones. Some Ayurvedic practitioners believe that synthetic stones work as well as natural ones; others do not. Ideally the stone should be cut and polished on the same day, but most buyers have no way of ascertaining this.

In Ayurveda, there are nine traditional gems, each with its own special quality and use. In general, red, yellow, and orange stones lower Vata and Kapha. Green and blue stones reduce Pitta. Purple stones balance all Doshas. For excellent all-round results, many people purchases bangles composed of all nine Ayurveda gems (*navaratnas*). These are considered to have powerful effects in nullifying bad karma.

It is fine to use a synthetic ruby or emerald in place of a natural one. Synthetic stones have the same chemical composition, and were created without resorting to the inhumane conditions that occur in many third-world mining operations.

Ruby: This is the stone of the Sun, and the king of gems. It is considered a life-protecting gem. Rubies come in a variety of red shades and the purer and richer the color, the more effective it will be. A clear, transparent stone is the most efficacious. Buy the stone on a Sunday, Monday, or Thursday during a time when the moon is waxing. You can get an excellent and large synthetic ruby for a fraction of the price as a natural stone. You can also use a garnet, but a synthetic ruby would be a better choice. If worn, it should be placed on the right side of the dog.

It is most efficacious for diabetes, anemia, fevers, and other blood problems, as well as digestive trouble and fevers. It will decrease Vata and Kapha (and is therefore most balancing for these doshas) and will increase Pitta very powerfully.

Pearl: The pearl is associated with the Moon and should have a moonlike, shining quality. Natural and cultured pearls are both used, but the natural pearl may be more efficacious. Pearls should be bought on Monday when the moon is waxing and set in silver. In Ayurveda the stone is said to provide strength, improved eyesight, mental calm, and is good for coughs, infertility, kidney disorders, and heart failure. It pacifies Pitta, but this gem is really balancing to all doshas. It also reduces aggression. A pearl with a reddish tint is said to increase intelligence. Some people make "pearl water" by allowing the gem to stand in a glass of water overnight. You can give the water to your dog the following day. Some authorities say it is quite acceptable to use a moonstone to replace a pearl. If worn it should be placed on the left side.

Yellow Sapphire: This is the stone of Jupiter. It should be a clear bright uniform color and of symmetrical shape. The stone should be bought on a Thursday and set in gold. It is said to confer groundedness. Yellow sapphire is beneficial for pets recovering from insect bites and other poisons, digestive ailments that produce vomiting, and liver troubles. It is a balancing stone and can be used equally well for all doshas, although it may slightly increase Kapha. If necessary, you can use yellow topaz or citrine to replace yellow sapphire, although the result may not be as satisfactory.

Zircon: While most people know the colorless zircon as a substitute for a diamond, in India, it is the yellow zircon which has the greatest value. It is symbolic of the shadowy planet Rahu. The best color, say the ancient texts, is the same color as cow's urine. Considering the esteem in which the cow is held in India, this may be taken as a compliment, but canary yellow or gold might be better in American culture. In some Ayurvedic therapy, yellow hessonite is used for zircon. It comes in several colors, as does zircon, but the yellow version is the one used in Ayurveda. The stone should be purchased on Saturday and set in gold. It improves skin quality, reproductive ability, and intelligence. It helps all doshas.

Emeralds: This is the stone of Mercury. It is not possible to find a flawless natural emerald, so do the best you can, or select a flawless synthetic. (Some synthetic emeralds include flaws on purpose to make them appear more natural, but you don't want flaws in a stone used for healing purposes.) Healing emeralds should be purchased on Wednesday and set in gold. Before use, the stone should be immersed overnight in cow's milk. This cooling gem is a great stone for Pitta and Vata illnesses, mental disorders, nervous diseases, abdominal pains, heart trouble, and fever. If a real emerald is too expensive you can use a synthetic emerald or an aquamarine.

Diamond: The diamond is associated with Venus, and should be bought on Friday. It should be set in white gold, silver, or platinum. The diamond energizes the life force and is an excellent stone for an animal recovering from electrical shock, heart problems, epilepsy, paralysis, hernia surgery, or psychological problems. Colorless diamonds reduce Pitta and increase Vata and Kapha. Red diamonds, on the other hand, tend to increase Pitta.

A white topaz can be used to replace the diamond if cost is an issue, although it is not as effective.

Moonstone: This mysterious stone belongs to the mystic, shadowy orb called Ketu in Indian astrology. It should be purchased on Wednesday, Thursday, or Friday morning when the moon is waxing. Ideally, it should be set in a mixture of iron, silver, copper, gold, and zinc.

This cooling stone is strongly linked with psychic ability and increases Vata, but is helpful to all doshas. Medicinally, it is used to increase physical strength, and helps cure wounds, skin diseases, and joint pain.

Blue Sapphire: The blue sapphire belongs to Saturn, and should be purchased on Saturday evening. It calms Vata and Kapha, and increases Pitta. It is considered a very spiritual stone. It is good for skin diseases, nervous disorders, skeletal system problems, and bloat.

Red Coral: Coral is identified with Mars and should be purchased on Tuesday. It gives courage, energy, and strength. It increases Pitta, according to most authorities. Others believe it lowers Pitta and Vata and raises Kapha, due to its association with water. It should be set in copper. It can be used in cases of dry coughs, arthritis, inflammations, eye problems, nursing dogs, and fever. Coral is a traditional Ayurvedic gem, but because of environmental reasons, it should be used with care.

Other stones, not included in the traditional nine, are also used from time to time in Ayurveda:

Amethyst: This is a good stone for mental clarity. It reduces Pitta and Vata. It should be set in gold. It is a stone of love, compassion, and hope and is the perfect stone for dogs who have been rescued.

Aquamarine: Aquamarine can be used as substitute for emerald. Both are beryls.

Jade: Jade is the stone for longevity. It helps the kidneys and is said to be useful for the prevention of cataracts.

Lapis Lazuli: Lapis is considered a spiritual stone that is generally tonifying. It calms Vata and Pitta and increases Kapha. It is good for eye ailments, liver, and skin diseases.

Opal: Opal is the stone of Neptune. It is said to strengthen the bone marrow and nerves (*majja dhatu*). It can be set in gold or silver. It is said to help vision, and calm Pitta.

Cat's Eye: This stone pacifies Kapha and Vata; it slightly increases Pitta. It is used for allergies and kidney dysfunction. It is said to protect from negative influences.

Onyx: This is a Vata reducing stone, that is especially good for older dogs, particularly those with canine cognitive dysfunction.

Quartz: Quartz reduces Vata and can sometimes be used as a diamond substitute. Rose quartz is especially good for this. Quartz is a good stone also to help you communicate with your dog. It can be set in silver or gold and should be placed on the right side of the dog.

The following is a traditional list of ailments and the appropriate Ayurvedic gem therapy:

Allergies: Cat's eye
Arthritis and other ***Musculo-skeletal Problems:*** Red coral, emerald, dark blue pearl
Blood Problems: Ruby, emerald, dark blue sapphire
Bone Disease: Sapphire and ruby
Diabetes: Red or white coral, emerald
Digestive Problems: red or white coral, emerald
Ear Problems: Yellow sapphire
Eye Problems: Lapis Lazuli, coral, opal, jade (cataracts)
Kidneys: Jade
Nervous System Disease: Dark blue sapphire
Psychological Problems: Emerald at night, coral during the day
Skin Disease: White coral, yellow sapphire

Gem Therapy by Dosha

Vata dogs respond best to amethyst, sapphire, yellow garnet, white moonstone, red or yellow opal, and to silver and gold.

Kapha dogs respond best to agate, red diamond, red and yellow garnet, red and yellow opal, ruby, topaz and to gold or copper.

In addition to their value as a setting for gems, metals have a unique place in Ayurvedic healing. The four most important healing metals are copper, gold, silver, and iron.

Metals

As a rule, the purer the metal, the more effective the healing will be. Pure gold is twenty-four carats; however, most American jewelry is set in only 14 karat gold. Indian jewelry is usually 18-karat gold.

Gold: Gold is important for both the heart and nervous system. It raises Pitta and reduces Kapha and Vata. In traditional Ayurvedic medicine, pure (24 karat) gold is placed in two cups of water and boiled down until half the liquid is gone. The remaining "gold water" is given by the teaspoon twice a day. The original gold is not destroyed by the cooking! Another traditional way of using gold is to place a piece of pure gold in a rice pot and cook as usual. The gold is then removed, and the rice is served.

The word "carat" is a measure of gem weight. Its cognate, "karat," measures the purity of gold. The "caret" is used to insert a missing word, and rabbits are fond of "carrots." This would all have been simple if people had been paying attention.

Iron: Iron is an important trace mineral in the body. It is present in every cell, but its greatest concentration is in oxygen carrying hemoglobin and myglobin. It is very helpful to the immune system, and strengthens the marrow. Cooking food in ironware is very helpful in ensuring your dog gets sufficient iron, although dogs receiving adequate amount of meat in their diets are unlikely to be iron-deficient.

Copper: Copper has the effect of reducing Kapha, and is traditionally used to ward off obesity. Copper is a vital trace element, being a component of many enzymes that catalyze reactions involving oxygen. It is essential for all cells and enables the incorporation of iron into hemoglobin. Copper affects skin and hair color by producing melanin, helps cartilage and connective tissue formation, helps cardiac function, myelinizes nerves, and promotes healing. It is found everywhere in the body, but is most concentrated in the brain, liver, heart, and kidney. In food, copper is found mostly in meat products. In Ayurvedic tradition, pouring pure water into a copper dish, allowing it to stand overnight and then serving the water is said to help anemia. It is also considered a good tonic for the liver, spleen, and lymphatic system.

Silver: Silver, a cooling metal that reduces excess Pitta and balances Vata. It is traditionally used to increase stamina. Silver water can be made by taking a small amount of pure silver and boiling it in two cups of water. Boil the liquid down to one cup and serve one teaspoon twice a day. It is said to help emaciation, weakness, and many intestinal problems.

Colors

Even though dogs don't perceive colors exactly the way people do, they are not colorblind. They are probably better at distinguishing shades of blue than we are, and since color is really nothing but light energy, color (even "invisible" colors) have an effect on them. The color of your dog's collar, sweater, bedding and similar items all have an effect upon his dosha.

Red: Red is a warm color that reduces Kapha and Vata. It increases Pitta, and promotes deep healing and energy. It is also good for blood formation and circulation. However, Pitta dogs who are over-exposed to red may be in danger of conjunctivitis and other inflammatory ailments.

Pink: Pink has similar but milder effects than red. It is also more calming than red, helps heal grief, and promotes relaxation. Pink may make Kapha dog lethargic, however.

Orange: Vibrant orange is warm and healing. It balances Kapha and Vata but can aggravate Pitta, just like red. This is a good color for dogs who are fighting infections; it is said to be anti-bacterial. It is also good for spleen, kidney, and lung ailments.

Yellow or ***Gold:*** Yellow reduces Vata and Kapha. It is good for dogs with kennel cough, as it is considered a decongestant. It is also good for nervous system problems.

Green: Calming, comforting green reduces Pitta but aggravates Kapha and Vata. It is said to help heal wounds and ulcers, and is good for the heart.

Blue: Blue reduces Pitta and aggravates Kapha and Vata. This anti-stress color is said to be good for disorders of the liver and all throat area problems.

Indigo: This balancing color is good for all senses, but especially vision, hearing, and the spiritual third eye. This is a color that increases stability in all dosha types.

Purple: Purple, a truly transformational color, increases Vata but balances Pitta and Kapha: It creates a lightness of body that is excellent for agile dogs.

Silver or ***Gray:*** This color is associated with the moon. It reduces Pitta and increases Kapha and Vata.

Some Ayurvedic practitioners use color by pouring pure water into a bottle made of the appropriate color and allowing bottle to sit out in the sun for a period of time – when cool, the water can be poured into the dog's bowl. If you do not have a bottle of the right color, you can wrap a clear bottle in colored cellophane. That will do as well.

Aromas

Aromas are well known to be helpful for certain conditions. Bronchitis and kennel cough for example, can be relieved by vapors or fragrances of basil, camphor, cedar, cinnamon, eucalyptus, frankincense, ajwan, gardenia, tumeric, ginger, iris, cardamom, jasmine, clove, lavender, lotus, mint, rose, rosemary, sandalwood, or myrrh. The oils have pretty much the same effect as the plants themselves. However, most of the time, aromas work more on the mind than they do on the body.

Aroma therapy can take many forms: incense, scented candles, sachets, and soaps. The best aromas are pure, with no chemical additives. In many cases a base or carrier oil is added to hold the scent. You can also place just a drop of the scented oil on the chest, paws, neck, or back of the skull. For Vata dogs, the best spot is in the head region, between the eyes, for Pitta dogs it is on the chest, and for Kapha dogs on the belly. The best carrier oil for your dog depends upon his dosha. Vata types do best with sesame oil, Pitta with sunflower, and Kapha with canola oil.

In general, sweet, warming, and earth aromas can balance an overactive Vata. The best Vata-balancing aromas include: Camphor (which has a warm after-effect), orange, clove, cardamom, lavender, cedar, pine, angelica, sandalwood, myrrh, and frankincense. You can also mix frankincense, basil, camphor or cinnamon with rose or sandalwood.

Cooling, sweet aromas like sandalwood, lotus, jasmine, rose, geranium, lemongrass, gardenia, and various mints are excellent soothers for Pitta.

Good scents for Kapha include camphor, eucalyptus, cinnamon, myrrh, frankincense, cedar, eucalyptus, thyme, basil, rosemary, and sage.

Specific Uses

Pain: myrrh or cinnamon
Cleansing: sandalwood or myrrh
Congestion: eucalyptus or sage
Digestion: cardamom or clove
Feet: peppermint oil in warm water
Immune system: myrrh, rose, or frankincense
Infections: eucalyptus or cedar
Air purification: camphor or frankincense
Rejuvenation: frankincense, myrrh, rose, or guggul
Soothing: sandalwood or rose
Stimulation: cardamom or fennel

Mantras and Music: Sound Therapy for the Ayurvedic Dog

Sound plays an important part in Ayurveda. The original Vedas were not written down, but sung and chanted. There are several reasons for this. The first and most obvious one is that most people were illiterate. A second reason is that the sages believed the Vedas were not self-explanatory. If they were written down and passed around like any other book, people would not seek guidance in understanding them. The guru-pupil relationship is a critical part of the Indian tradition, and the ancients believed that literature, spoken or written, was the start and not the end of knowledge. In addition, sound itself was understood to have a powerful effect on healing and insight. Part of the healing process was believed to be located in the mantras, or short chants of empowering syllables. There existed no accurate system of musical notation, so unless the pupil heard the mantra (and not just read it) its effect could be reduced. To this day, the most powerful mantras are not written down, but passed orally from the master to the pupil.

While your dog should not be expected to chant a mantra, you can! Healing mantras quietly recited over your dog will bring him peace and healing. There are two basic kinds of mantras: a seed mantra and a Shabda mantra.

A seed mantra is a collection of symbols that have no specific meaning, although many have been used for centuries. The power of the mantra comes from the vibratory power of the sound alone. This energy represents the power of the Ultimate (what westerners sometimes call God).

A Shabda Mantra is a meaningful sentence, often containing praise or petition. Many come from the Vedas, the sacred books of India.

A mantra is recited many times (often 108 times) with a pause between each repetition. This pause is very important, and represents the "unstruck" chord, or essential, vibrant silence at the core of the universe. (The number 108 is a sacred number in both the Hindu and Buddhist traditions, and prayer beads traditionally have 108 beads on them. Even the Nepalese Parliament has 108 seats. However, why 108 is such a magical-sacred number is lost in antiquity. In other words, no one has a clue, although there are plenty of guesses.)

Here are some of the most famous one-word healing mantras that you can use separately or put together creatively to make your own seed mantra. The syllables for the most part have no individual meaning.

Aum: the ultimate syllable. The most powerful word in any mantra is "Aum." Each letter is pronounced separately, with a slight pausing breath after the word. The "a" sound represents the creation of the universe as you open your mouth to speak the word. The "u" sound represents the maintenance and preservation of this same cosmos. And the "m" sound symbolizes the inevitable destruction of the universe. The following pause represents the hiatus before the cosmos recreates itself, forever and ever. This is a mind-altering mantra that empowers all others. Recite with your hand on the dog's head. This is a good mantra for Pitta and Kapha dogs, especially.

Aym: This mantric syllable is sacred to the goddess of wisdom, Saraswati. It improves concentration and is excellent for dogs in event training. A good mantra for Pitta and Kapha dogs.

Ham: This mantric syllable stands for the element ether and energizes the respiratory system. Recite with your hand on the dog's throat.

Hoom: "Hoom" is a sound said to be sacred to Shiva, the Hindu god of destruction. This mantric syllable is believed to ward off negative influences, burn Ama and clear channels. This is a great mantra for both Vata and Kapha dogs.

Hrim: This is a cleansing and purifying mantra. It is a great detoxifier for animals who are recovering from poisoning. It also is good for use while cleaning kennels and other areas.

Klim: This Kapha-increasing mantra provides strength and emotional control for dogs that are excessively angry or fearful.

Krim: This mantra is empowering for action, and is often used while preparing Ayurvedic herbs. It is great to use at the start of dog events such as a conformation show, tracking, field trials, or agility tests.

Ksham: This mantra gives peace, and is connected with the "third eye." Recite with your fingers on the dog's forehead, above and between his eyes.

Lam: Lam is the "earth" mantra and is excellent for problems of the excretory system. Recite with your hand on the dog's hindquarters.

Ram (pronounced with a long "ah" sound): "Ram" is probably the second most powerful mantric syllable. It is the name of Rama, an avatar of the preserving god Vishnu (an avatar is the appearance of a god on earth in a new form). This mantra brings strength, and peace and it is ideal for calming mental disturbances and fears. Medicinally, it is said to strengthen ojas and build the immune system. This is an excellent mantra for Vata dogs.

Ram (pronounced with a short "u" sound): Ram is the fire mantra and increases will, energy, and motivation. Recite with your hand on the dog's abdomen.

Sham: This is the peace mantra (the related Sanskrit word Shanti means peace). It creates calm, alleviates stress, and is said to be good for chronic degenerative nervous system disorders. Excellent for Pitta dogs.

Shrim: This mantra is said to promote overall health. It is especially good for the plasma and reproductive fluids. Like Krim, this is a good mantra to recite when preparing herbs. It is superior for Pitta dogs.

Shum: This sound increases vitality and fertility.

Som (rhymes with home): This sound is a general tonic for the whole system.

Vam: Vam is the water mantra and helps the reproductive system.

Yam: This "air" mantra helps the heart, clears the circulatory system, and provides all-around energy. Recite with your hand on the dog's chest.

Before using the mantras directly on your dog, purify the healing area by reciting ***Aum*** and ***Hoom*** several times.

Music

Like the mantras, music therapy has become an important part of the Ayurvedic system. Western medicine is finally catching up to the idea that music can be healing, and it is now an accepted adjunct therapy in many hospitals around the country. There's an old story that the Indian master musician Thyagaraja brought a dead person back to life with one of his compositions, but that's a little much to expect even from Ayurveda!

In Indian music, the basic melody or form is known as the raga. About 75,000 classical ragas exist, each grouped under 10 "parent scales." Each raga has its own mood and healing power, and is ideally played at a certain time of day or season of the year. Some are very specific – one of them – the Ahir Bhairav is to be played only when the very first ray of the sun is spotted at dawn. Indian classical instruments include the dhapli, dholak, duff, flute, sitar, shahnai, tablas, and mridangum.

In scientific terms, it is believed that music stimulates the pituitary gland, which in turn controls many aspects of the nervous and metabolic systems. Most people have discovered that the right kind of music can ease pain, cure headaches, and dispel anger. There is no reason to suppose it acts differently with dogs. The key is to find the right music for your dog's dosha. Ayurvedic musicians have produced music to raise or lower the various doshas, so it is up to you to decide what needs to be balanced. You can purchase such music almost anywhere, even on Amazon.com.

Massage and Touch Therapy

Massage is part of the traditional rejuvenation and detoxification program used in Indian medicine. In Ayurvedic theory, aches and pains are caused by obstruction of the flow of wind (*vayu*) through vayu-carrying channels (*siras*). Massage encourages the bodily airs to expand and to move, thus generating healing heat, and removing tension. It also helps develop a deeper, more natural breathing pattern and promotes an electrochemical balance in the body.

The best-known Ayurvedic massage technique, at least for humans, is Abhyanga or whole body massage. Combined with an individually-prepared herbal oil, it penetrates deeply. This massage is designed to help expel waste-matter from the body, stimulates circulation, and helps nutrients reach the cells. As with all massage, it helps move Vayu (air) through its channels more efficiently. This reduces pain, decreases tensions, and helps build up body heat. In dogs you can gently massage along his torso. If the dog seems uncomfortable or tries to resist, stop. If, as is most likely, he closes his eyes and falls asleep, you may continue the massage up to 20 minutes or so. Generally your hands will follow the contours of the body in the direction that the hair flows (or alternatively, in the direction of the circulation). There is a great deal of complexity to proper Ayurvedic massage, depending on the movement of the sub-doshas. In most cases, only a skilled Ayurvedic practitioner can give the ultimate healing massage. That being said, it's important to note that any gentle massage is healthful, except in the cases of infection, wounds, and tumors.

Special attention is paid to the *marma* points, energy points grouped according to the region of the body – legs, abdomen, back, head, and neck. They are also grouped according muscles, tendons/ligaments, arteries/veins, joints, and bones. As these points are somewhat different on each type of dog, it is best to work with an experienced Ayurvedic practitioner to locate them.

Another massage technique, *Vishesh,* is a deep-muscle massage therapy that helps break up adhesions within the muscle. It should be performed only by a dog-knowledgeable Ayurvedic practitioner.

In human massage, certain fragrant oils are frequently used to help the massage and nourish the skin. According to Vagbhata, the founder of Ayurvedic massage, the proper oil depends upon the season. With dogs, however, it is not practical or usually advisable to pour oil on the fur as the washing away of it in a bath is usually stressful to dogs and could vitiate any benefits therefrom. A commercial product, Groom Dog Liquid Calm Massage Oil, is also available. Simply use a judicious amount on the paws, inside the ear earflaps, or other comparatively hairless area and wipe it away gently. Only a few drops on the chest or neck are needed. Neroli, or roman chamomile is commonly used.

Use gentle circular strokes. A skilled Ayurvedic practitioner knows how to use massage to maximize the flow of the five energies (earth, water, fire, air, and ether) through the body for optimum effect by varying the rate, pressure and placement of strokes, but a gentle fingertip massage done by the owner is always beneficial.

Indian massage spends a lot of time on the head; many "vital points" are located right beneath the scalp. Then time is spent on the ears, neck (front and back), shoulders, upper back, front legs, chest, chest abdomen, and feet which are too often neglected. The general massage lasts from ten to fifteen minutes.

The proper oil to use is largely dependent on the dosha of the dog, although your choice may also depend what specific condition you are trying to treat. In general, the correct oils for each dosha are as follows:

- Vata dogs – sesame seed or almond oil
- Kapha dogs – small amount of sesame seed or corn oil
- Pitta dogs – coconut or sunflower oil

Therapeutic massage oils can be made from amla, bhami, bhringaraj and neem. Neem oil should be used only in a diluted form, as the pure extract is too strong. More details are given in chapter 8.

Chapter 7

Exercise, Yoga, Breathing and Meditation

Exercise and Your Dog

Mind and body go together, therefore so do meditation and exercise. Proper meditation can prepare the body for action and good exercise calms and focuses the mind.

For dogs exercise is the natural way to enter into their primal being. They evolved to be chasers, herders, hunters, and workers. Giving your modern-day dog a chance to participate in activities that recall his ancient heritage makes your dog a more natural and better pet. It is true that tiny dogs like Chihuahuas were bred mostly to be companion dogs and can get most of the exercise they need by charging around the apartment. Even larger dogs bred to be guard dogs don't require as much running exercise as you might imagine. However, herding dogs, hunting dogs, and working dogs thrive on an hour or more aerobic exercise every day. Vata and Pitta dogs are naturals for exercise (and many even self-exercise) but even the gentle couch potato Kapha dog enjoys it – and probably needs it – although she may sleep all day on the couch if you allow it.

Exercise has another benefit as well – it creates bonding between dogs and their owners.

Equally important, exercise is a natural weight control system that your dog loves! Obesity is a growing problem among dogs, and should properly be called animal abuse. Obesity is bad for the joint, lungs, and heart, and it doesn't do much for an animal's mental well being either. Although dogs are not concerned about trying to squeeze into a size 4, they do enjoy being fit enough to run, play catch, fetch sticks, and chase each other around a field. All of those things become increasingly difficult for the overweight dog. Eventually walking around becomes too difficult, so they stop even that. Thus, they move less and less and get fatter and fatter. Eventually even breathing becomes too difficult and they die.

If this happens it is your fault, not the dog's. Unlike his wild forbears, the modern domestic dog no longer has caribou to run down if he wants to eat. Instead his dinner is carried to him on a platter or bowl. You probably don't want your dog running wild through the neighborhood, but it is important that he gets an equivalent amount of exercise. You are the one in charge of his diet and exercise. Get him moving. Studies show, by the way, that dog owners who walk their dogs regularly also lose weight themselves! Get started!

Exercise is most important for Kapha-type dogs. Like all dogs, they need physical exercise every day – and you have to make sure he gets it, because Kapha dogs, unlike some other types, are definitely not self exercisers! These dogs also improve dramatically when taken to obedience or even agility classes where they can exercise their minds as well as their bodies. If you don't exercise them, they will become torpid and dull.

Yoga

However, while meditation is an essential part of Ayurveda for human beings, you can't expect your Chihuahua to assume a full-lotus position and begin to concentrate upon the divine spark within. And he doesn't have to. Meditation is for you. And you'll both benefit.

Meditation will make you calmer, more peaceful, and more in tune with yourself. That will make you a better dog owner.

One type of Indian meditation is often called Yoga. Yoga means "yoke" or "union" and its purpose is to connect the meditator with the divine force within and without. Its benefits are physical, mental, and spiritual. In the physical sphere, it detoxifies the body and balances the three doshas. In the mental arena, it clarifies, calms, and focuses the mind. And spiritually, it deepens and broadens the soul.

Contrary to popular belief, yoga doesn't require bizarre postures and hours of impenetrable silence. You don't have to buy a leotard or sit on the floor. You don't need to spend a penny on equipment, and many classes are even free. In a world where religion is largely for sale, you can go yogic without worrying about money for the collection box, expensive "Sunday clothes," or finding a nearby church. Clothes need only be loose and comfortable (and some people even practice nude). You can practice alone, with friends, or join a class. This is an infinitely "portable" activity! It has no creed to conflict with anyone's religious beliefs and no dogma that would violate anyone's moral principles.

Yoga has indeed become deservedly popular. It's estimated that over 18 million Americans are currently doing some form of yoga. And above them all is Raja-yoga, the king of yoga, a spiritual discipline that attempts to unify the practitioner with the Ultimate. This practice incorporates many aspects of the other yogas, including self-control, religious observances, physical postures, breath control, withdrawal of sense-consciousness, deep concentration, one-pointed meditation, leading finally to a superconscious state that is identified as union with the divine. If you have arrived at this point, you have achieved the holy state of the divine: *satchitananada* – Being, Knowledge, and Bliss, the union of body, mind, and spirit, the foci of the three classical yogas.

But your yoga ambitions don't have to be so lofty. Yoga is as effective for people looking for self-knowledge and stress relief as it is for emaciated ascetics who seek absolute liberation from mortal life. Yoga today is one of the most diversified practices on earth, and yoga practitioners come from every religious and philosophical tradition.

And while yoga is sometimes associated (in this country at least) with lithe young women in little black leotards, men may benefit even more from the practice than women do. After a lifetime of stiff-upper lipping and over-control of feelings, men find in yoga a disciplined yet comfortable way to relax and express emotions in a calm, freeing way.

Like life itself, yoga begins with the breath, which is the embodied spirit. The steady breath supports both the body and the mind. For example, yoga has been used successfully to treat depression. *The Journal of Affective Disorders* published a review of five studies measuring the effects of yoga practice on depression between January and June of 2004. The review considered only yoga practices that included pranayama breathing and relaxation techniques. (Three of the studies included breathing practices and relaxation only.) All five randomized control trials reported positive outcomes for populations with mild to severe depression. No adverse effects were reported, except for fatigue and breathlessness in participants in one study.

And special yogic breathing may have another benefit. One common technique used is breathing through one nostril at a time. And, oddly enough, electroencephalogram (EEG) studies of the electrical impulses in the brain have revealed that when you breathe through one nostril, there is increased electrical activity on the opposite side of the brain. It may be that the regular practice of breathing through one nostril may improve communication between the right and left lobes of the brain. Integration, indeed, is what yoga is all about. It reconnects you to your own inner power.

And it helps the physical body as well. Studies suggest that yoga is beneficial for such diverse conditions as diabetes, hypertension, digestive disorders, arthritis, menstrual disorders, arteriosclerosis, chronic fatigue, asthma, varicose veins, and heart conditions. Yogic relaxation techniques and meditation can also help reduce chronic pain. Back pain, for instance, is one of the most common reasons people seek medical attention. (Perhaps we were never intended to walk upright.) Yoga has been used to reduce or eliminate back pain by enhancing strength and flexibility, and by reducing stress, a major component of back trouble. For arthritis sufferers, the slow-motion movements of yoga and its gentle stretches relieve the tightness and pain in affected joints. It is also a purifier (or in today's language, a "detoxifier") that cleanses the body totally. The outer results are clear, glowing skin and bright eyes, but the real benefits are in the unseen internal organs.

Yoga can be preventive as well as curative. It appears to create a balance between the nervous and endocrine systems which in turns controls all the other systems and organs of the body. Pulse and respiratory rates decrease. Blood pressure drops. Cardiovascular efficiency and stamina increase through the "continuity of action," or *vinyasa* postures. Execratory functions improve. Grip strength increases. Reaction time improves. Immune function increases. Eye-hand coordination improves. Balance gets better. Yoga practice results in a decrease of sodium, total cholesterol, triglycerides, and catecholamines, but an increase of hematocrit, hemoglobin, thyroxin, and total serum protein.

Many have also found yoga helpful for weight reduction. (You've never seen a fat swami, have you?) Many yoga postures (*asanas*), such as the "fish" and the "shoulder stand," stimulate the thyroid gland, which in turn affects body metabolism. Yogic deep breathing also increases fat metabolism by increasing oxygen intake to the cells. Deep breathing also tends to burn many of the calories you've already ingested! In addition, yoga reduces anxiety and the over-eating that may accompany it. Besides all this, almost all yogic practitioners recommend a natural and moderate diet for best results (and best all around heath). The results are less fat, more muscle, and a leaner, fitter you. (You don't have to become a vegetarian or even give up smoking, although you know you probably should.)

Regular yoga practice also has psychological implications. It improves mood, decreases anxiety and hostility, increases attention and memory functions, and definitely adds increased self-awareness.

Finding time for yoga is partly dependent on your work schedule, but you will discover that both morning and evening sessions have their benefits. Practicing in the morning before breakfast (but after your shower) will prepare you for a whole day of work or play, while an evening session around sunset can relieve the stress that may have piled up during the day.

However, while the benefits of yoga are universally acknowledged, it's a good idea to look before you leap. Not everyone who has completed a weekend course in yoga is qualified to be a teacher of this subtle discipline. The Yoga Alliance recommends that a yoga teacher should have at least 200 hours of expert training. Before taking a class, ask about the credentials of the instructor. A bad teacher is worse than ineffective – she can cause serious harm. Medical practitioners are seeing more and more yoga-related cases of muscle and ligament sprains, neck and back pain, and cartilage tears, most of them a result of poor teaching. Psychological and spiritual disturbances, though, not as obvious, can be equally severe.

But when yoga is taught right, it's golden. Each yoga practice is a totally new experience, opening a new vista and a world of new possibilities. There's a specific yoga for everyone, including you. As long as you can breathe, you can practice.

Classic Yoga Asanas

There are hundreds of different *asanas* or yogic postures. In fact, one Indian text asserts that there at 84 million seated *asanas* alone, not to mention all the other kinds.

Here are just a few of them. Many of them incorporate other poses. For best results, though, join a yoga class. Despite the popularity of "Doga," your canine will benefit much more if you just take the class yourself.

Child's Pose (Bala Asana) Difficulty Level 1.

This simple, pure pose is extremely calming. Put your hands palms down on your thighs. Sit on your feet with your feet together but pointed outward, and your knees hip-width apart. Your backside is resting on your heels. (This alone is called the Thunderbolt Pose.)

1. Breathe in deeply and the exhale, lowering your chest to your knees and swinging your arms forward. Let your forehead rest on the floor if possible. Then bring your arms back so that they are lying on the outside of each leg, palms up.
2. Hold the pose for one or two minutes, breathing quietly. Then return to position 1. Repeat two or three times.

Corpse Pose (Shava Asana) Difficulty Level 1.

The biggest physical danger in this Asana is the risk that you might fall asleep!

1. Lie flat on your back with your legs together but not touching. Your arms should be straight alongside your body with the palms upwards.
2. Close your eyes and breathe gently.
3. Concentrate on relaxing each part of your body while you breathe quietly. If you feel yourself getting tired, breathe more deeply and at a quicker pace.

Serpent Pose (Bhjangsana) Difficulty level 1.5.

This pose helps digestion and raises awareness.

1. Lie on your stomach with your hands parallel to your shoulders, palms on the floor.
2. Breathe in, and raise your head and upper torso. Let your back muscles, not your hands, do the lifting. Your lower torso and legs stay on the ground.
3. Exhale, and lower yourself gently to the ground.

Half-Moon Pose (Ardhachandra Asana) Difficulty Level 2.

This is an excellent balancing and stretching pose.

1. Stand with your feet touching, keeping your back straight and your arms against your the sides, palms facing inward. This is the *Tada Asana* or Mountain Pose, and the starting point for many yogic exercises.
2. Bring your hands together at your chest in the salutation or prayer gesture *(Anjali Mudra).*
3. Breathe in and bring your arms straight up with the palms still pressed together.
4. Arch backwards, still keeping your upper arms along side your head and neck. Tilt your head back and hold. Your knees should be straight. Breathe slowly.
5. Return to the beginning Tada posture.

Hero's Pose (Virasana) Difficulty Level 2.

This pose strengthens the whole body and develops courage. It is considered to be good for immune disorders.

1. Sit on your left heel. Bend the right knee, placing the right foot by the left knee.
2. Place your left elbow on your right knee with the palm of your left hand against your right cheek.
3. Pace your right palm on your left knee.
4. Close your eyes and concentrate on your breath.

Fish Pose (Matsya Asana) Difficulty Level 3.

This is a great pose to do if you are suffering from a congested chest or sinus trouble; it opens everything right up.

1. Lie flat on your back as in the Corpse Pose (above).
2. Keep your backside on the floor, breathe in, and raise your head, shoulders, back, and upper arms off the floor, arching your back and opening out the chest.
3. Tilt your head back and place the top of your head on the floor.
4. Raise your elbows off the the floor and bring your hands in a prayer-like gesture *(anjali mudra),* just below the chest. The fingers should be pointing upwards.
5. Hold for a breath or so. Return to the Corpse Pose.

Sun Salute (Surya Namaskar) Difficulty Level 4.

This is one of the most sacred Yoga exercises, with a mid-level difficulty. It is particularly useful in avoiding stress. If you have time for only one yoga posture a day, this should be the one! It stretches all the muscle groups, boosts the respiratory system, and symbolically honors that most important object (or god, in the Hindu view) the Sun.

1. Stand straight with your feet together and your palms pressed (as in prayer) in front of your chest. Relax and inhale.
2. Then separate your hands and raise your arms in a wide circle out to the sides and above your head. Stretch your arms back to let your chest expand to the fullest. Then press your palms together above your head. Look up at your hands and stretch towards them. Hold your breath and the pose for a few seconds.
3. Exhale and bend forward from the waist, palms together, head tucked, with back as straight as possible.
4. Reach down and hold your ankles (or as far as you can reach). Keep your head as close to the body as you can. Let your breath out and hold it out for a few seconds.
5. Inhale and stand up again. Breathe out and lunge forward with your right leg, supporting your weight on your hands, your

right foot, left knee, and toes of your left foot. Tilt your head back and look up. Hold your breath. (When you repeat the exercise, reverse legs.)

6. Breathe in and raise your arms again in a wide circle as in step 3. Hold for a few seconds.
7. Exhale and place both hands on the floor on either side of your right foot. Stretch your right foot back next to your left foot and straighten your body. (You should resemble a board at this point. Keep saying to yourself – "It's all for the dog; it's all for the dog.")
8. Hold your breath out and lower your body so that chin, chest, and knees all touch the floor (toes are still tucked under). Then relax and inhale.
9. Continue breathing in and curl your head back. Lift your chest and stomach, but keep your hips on the floor. This is the cobra pose and you should feel like a snake.
10. Exhale and raise hips up and heels down, so that you are in an inverted "V" position. Tuck your chin to your chest. Keep holding your breath out.
11. Breathe in, straighten up and return to the posture in step 1.
12. Repeat a few times.

Pranayama (Breathing Exercises)

After you have finished your yoga exercises, it's time to sit quietly for some healthful deep breathing, or *pranayama,* which literally means "breath control." Practice includes controlled inhalation, exhalation, and breath retention.

The ancient Indian seers noticed a close connection between breathing and the mind, aside from the obvious one that if you can't breathe, you can't think. We all have been told to "take a deep breath" when we are in danger of "losing it." There's a good reason for this advice. Breathing is closely related to the brain and central nervous system. In addition, certain areas of the mucus membrane in the nose are connected to the internal organs such as the heart, lungs, and kidneys.

A deep breath calms the nerves, and gives your brain a little more oxygen. This enables you to make better, calmer choices. Incorporating a session of proper breathing every day helps tune your brain and nerves for the stresses to come. The results will be a calmer, more capable dog-owner, who in turn transmits less stress to her dog.

There is an old yogic idea that those who breathe less frequently will live longer. While that may or may not be true, rapid, excited breathing usually indicates a flustered state that is certainly not good for your health!

Everyone has noticed how sometimes the airflow seems to pass more easily through one nostril and sometimes through the other. Pranayana techniques make use of this basic physiological fact. The left side of the brain is associated with the right nostril, and vice versa. The left brain is the "male" side and it is associated with logic, aggression, and critical judgments. The right brain is the"female" and is associated with emotion, intuition and compassion. Everyone needs to cultivate both sides, otherwise there wouldn't be much use in having a brain.

Ayurvedic practitioners believe the prana that flows through the nadis or channels in the body is stored in the chakras or energy centers that exist along the spinal column. There are several such chakras (authorities differ on precisely how many). The purpose of controlled breathing, as in yoga, is to help release the stored energy upward to the highest chakra, the crown chakra, from which it is freed to join the infinite.

It is best not to eat for one hour before practicing pranayana.

Remember these techniques are for you, not for your dog. Any attempt you may make to force your dog into breathing exercises will only stress him and have the opposite effect from what you want. If you notice your dog panting abnormally or having labored breathing, he is in distress. Use gentle, calming tones and stroking to restore his normal breathing rhythm. Take him to a veterinarian if needed.

Alternate Breathing *(Nadi Shodana)*

Alternate nostril breathing is a way to "charge" both sides of the brain. Choose a quiet moment, and sit comfortably on the floor or firm chair with both feet flat on the floor.

1. Close your right nostril with your thumb, and rest your index and middle finger on the "third eye" in the center of the forehead. Breathe deeply – all the way into your abdomen (of course your breath only goes as far as your lungs, but a good deep breath will feel as if it is going into the abdomen).
2. Hold your breath for a second or two, while keeping your thumb on your right nostril.
3. Exhale slowly through your left nostril.

Then reverse the procedure. Repeat for several minutes. Concentrate on the movement of your breath. This technique is particularly beneficial to increase Vata.

Cooling Breath *(Shitali)*

If you are one of the people who can curl their tongue into a tube, do so. Inhale slowly through the tongue-tube, swallow, and exhale through the nose, with your mouth closed. If you can't curl your tongue (it's not your fault – it's genetic), simply clench your teeth, with your tongue pressed against either the upper or lower row (not both – because them you won't be able to breathe at all) and take in the air through your mouth. You should immediately notice the cooling effect, and indeed this is an exercise designed to pacify Pitta. Repeat several times.

Breath of Fire *(Bhastrika Pranyama)*

This is a warming breath designed to increase Pitta. Inhale the normal way, but exhale with more force than usual. Begin slowly, and then exhale more actively with some force. Repeat for 30 breaths, then rest. Repeat again up to five more times.

Hissing Breath

This is a cooling breath that should be practiced only in the summer. Sit comfortably with your eyes closed and your body erect. Bring your chin down to your chest. Clench your teeth and open your lips. Inhale slowly, listening to the hiss the air makes as you draw it in. Close your mouth and exhale through the nose. Repeat 20 times. The old rishis say this breath exercise will help you develop the qualities of divine love!

Humming Breath *(Bhramari Pranayama)*

Most people find this exercise impossible to perform in its pure form. You are instructed to begin a hum, and inhale and exhale. The hum is supposed to change tones on inhalation and exhalation. However, since it is physiologically impossible for most people to hum upon inhalation, simply take a deep breath and hum on exhalation. Keep the tip of the tongue against the edge of the soft palate and do not clench your teeth. This is a kind of sound therapy.

Victory Breath *(Ujjayi Pranayama)*

Sit in the Vajrayana or Lotus asana if you can. Otherwise you can sit in a straight chair. Sit straight and place your chin on your chest. Concentrate on your throat. Pretend you are going to swallow something – but don't. Stop just before the gulp – with the trachea pressed upward, almost as if you were going to say the letter "e." Then inhale deeply and slowly all the way down. Hold for a moment and then exhale slowly in the same way. You will hear a deep, slow rushing sound. Don't grunt. This is longevity breathing and it excellent for all dosha types.

Breath Meditation I: The Empty Bowl

In this simple combination of breathing technique and meditation, you need no special space or equipment. You can practice it anywhere – even right before a dog show! Simply sit quietly. You do not need to contort yourself into the lotus position, which Indians find relaxing, but most westerners, accustomed to chairs, find painful or even excruciating. (Chairs are a relatively recent invention, believe it or not, and most ancient Indians simply didn't own one.)

The meditation starts with simply breathing – and paying attention to each breath. Your mouth should be just slightly open. Feel each breath as it enter and leaves – and then follow it. Follow your indrawn breath as it passes into your lungs and then out again into the universe. Understand that breathing is simply borrowing from the universe and giving back to it. The universe sustains you with every breath, holds you, and then draws back again like a ceaseless tide. Practice for about 15 minutes morning and evening.

Why is it called the Empty Bowl? In one way, an empty bowl seems useless, but if you think about it, only the empty can be filled. It is vibrant with waiting. You too are an empty bowl, tremendously alive, waiting to be filled by the universe.

Breath Meditation *II: So-Hum*

This meditation is like the empty bowl, except that you add sound. When you inhale, utter the simple sibilant syllable "So," the sound that wind makes rustling through the trees, enters your body. Hold for just a second. As you exhale, make the sound "hum" The "so" stands for the cosmic Self, the "hum" for the small individual self. "So" is considered by some the sound of inhalation and "hum" the sound of exhalation. During this exercise you are breathing in the divine cosmic spirit and breathing out the petty, small self. It is usually repeated 108 times, a symbolically significant number in Indian tradition. The ideal rate is 6.5 breaths per minute, so the whole practice should take about 17 minutes. The "hum" sound is a little longer than the "so" part. Do not pause between breaths, and try for a smooth transition. Breathe with the diaphragm, which is just below the breast bone. Do twice a day.

These practices are not meant to be a complete list of breathing exercises. There are dozens. Choose one of the above that makes you feel comfortable, refreshed, and reinvigorated.

You don't actually need to say the syllables aloud, although it is preferable. You can also imagine them.

Rest and Sleeping

Rest is just as important as exercise for the maintenance of a healthy lifestyle. Modern dogs generally don't have any trouble getting enough sleep, but the quality of that sleep is really critical. And the quality of sleep depends not so much on an expensive bed, but upon where that bed is. Dogs are pack animals, and in the kingdom of their cousins the wolves, being separated from the pack to sleep alone is a sign of ostracism. It is an emotional stressor that can weaken his spirit. It is against his nature. Your dog does not have to sleep in your bed (that can be a stressor to you) but he should be allowed to sleep in your room next to your bed in his own basket.

Beds, especially for puppies, ill, and elderly animals, should also be placed out of drafts and direct sunlight in summer.

Chapter 8

Ailments and Treatment

In this section I discuss several common problems seen in dogs and possible Ayurvedic treatment for them. Remember, though, how important getting the correct diagnosis is. The wrong diagnosis can lead to the wrong treatment, which may make the problem worse, not better. You also have several options for most treatments, including mainstream veterinary care. It's not wise to pile up cures, thinking that more is better than less. Choose the most conservative remedy first. If one remedy doesn't work, seek out a different one, taking into account your dog's personal dosha. Some ingredients work well on one dosha but not on another, but if you are unsure, check the herb guide in chapter 5.

Also never neglect the critical role of diet, exercise, and lifestyle. If you cure a disease but do nothing to eliminate or ameliorate the causative agent, the problem will just come back – and then it may be worse.

Illness can be explained in many ways. Conventional western terminology is one way and Ayurvedic language is another. Interestingly, both systems often agree on the right course of action and sometimes on the same principles.

Be patient. Most traditional remedies are designed to work slowly over a period of time. They are not instant fixes. Chronic conditions take a long time to build up, and may also take a long time to clear.

Because Ayurvedic medicine was developed in a simpler time, traditional remedies do not have the same efficacy as many modern treatments do. That is not to say they don't work, but it does mean that they work more slowly than modern medicine. *Sometimes, you cannot afford to wait.* If you use the common-sense principles of Ayurveda along with regular professional veterinary care, your dog will benefit from both systems.

In an emergency such as bloat, trauma, seizures, paralysis, severe bloody diarrhea, or glaucoma, take your dog to the emergency animal hospital right away.

Abdominal Distention

Abdominal distention is not normal. It is not a disease in itself, but a sign that something else is wrong. Any change in the normal size and shape of your dog's abdomen can be a cause for alarm. A dog with a swollen abdomen may just be getting fat, but it could also be a sign of bloat, liver problems, infection, tumor, or an obstruction in the urinary tract. These are all extremely dangerous conditions, and in the case of bloat (see below) can result in agonizing pain within hours – or less. Before you embark on a course of Ayurvedic treatment for a *symptom,* get a diagnosis as to *cause.*

Allergies

An allergy is simply a hyper-reaction to a substance (normally a protein). Dogs are prone to many different sorts of allergies, just as people are. They can be allergic to pollen, dust, grass, and even different sorts of food. Unlike people, however, most dog allergies manifest themselves in the skin and coat rather than in the respiratory system. This is especially true of Pitta dogs. Dogs with allergies tend to scratch, lose hair, and develop ear infections. Go to a qualified practitioner to determine the source of the allergy, and, if possible eliminate it from the environment.

Behavioral Management: Reduce stress.

Diet: Use a Pitta-pacifying diet for skin allergies, even if your dog is not a Pitta type.

Herbs:

- Herbal local treatment may include frankincense, jatamansi, neem oil in a sesame base, titkta ghrita (bitter ghee), or sandalwood.
- For Vata and Kapha allergies to pollens: Take trikatu (dry ginger, black pepper and pippali powder in equal amounts) 10 mgm. + basil 125 mgm. + 5 mgm. each of cloves, camphor, and

coriander. It is advisable to take this mixture 2 times a day with warm water and food.
- Try this herbal mixture as a tea twice a day over your dog's food: 8 parts shatavari, 1 part gudachi, and 1/4 part shanka bhasma.
- For a good blood cleanser, mix equal parts of manjustha and neem and give a quarter of a teaspoon twice a day. If you can't obtain this combination, the western herb burdock has the same effect.
- Combination herbal: Triphala is good for all sorts of allergies. Give 1/2 teaspoonful at night.

Gems: Cat's eye is the gem for allergies.

Anemia

Anemia is a condition of the blood in which the red-cell blood count is below normal. The pulse will be faint and only felt at intervals. The blood count is the definitive test for anemia, but Ayurvedic medicine recognizes a different approach that depends on the dog's dosha. Like other diseases, anemia manifests itself as a Vata, Pitta, or Kapha type. The Vata type shows itself in rough, scaly skin, breathlessness, and perhaps tarry stools. The Pitta type shows itself in darker urine, yellowish stool, or pain in the abdomen. In Pitta dogs the problem may be due to an overbalance of *Ranjaka,* a sub-dosha of Pitta. Give a Pitta-reducing diet and herbs. Kapha anemia may be accompanied by swelling.

Dogs with all types of anemia need to eat iron-rich foods. They also do well with yogurt (include a little turmeric) twice a day.

Vata-type Anemia can be treated by:
- Tikta ghrita (bitter ghee). Half a teaspoon twice a day.
- Herbal mixture of 2 parts kaishore guggulu, 1/8 parts abrak bhasma, 5 parts ashwagandha, and 5 parts dashamoola. Give 1/4 teaspoon of the mixture twice a day.
- Iron and/or folic acid supplementation.

Pitta-type Anemia can be treated by:
- Cooking a mixture of ghee and shatavari together. One teaspoon twice a day.
- Mixing 5 parts shatavari, 3 parts brahmi, 2 parts neem and 1/8 part loha bhasa (an iron-containing compound). Give a quarter of a teaspoon 2 times a day.

- Some dogs may respond to vitamin B-12 (cobalamine supplements) as well as blue-green algae (spirulina) supplementation.

Pitta-type anemia may be associated with liver problems. Try serving his water in a copper bowl (leave overnight in the fridge before serving).

Kapha-type Anemia can be treated by

- 5 parts punarnava, 3 parts gokshura and 2 parts kutki. Give one or two teaspoons once a day.

Dogs with Kapha type anemia may do well with more high-quality protein in the diet. Try serving his water in a copper bowl (leave overnight in the fridge before serving).

Beneficial Color: Red

Anxiety

Dogs suffer from anxiety, especially separation anxiety, just as people do. We have bred dogs to be companion animals who are dependent upon us for their food and well-being. Therefore, it should not come as a shock when they become distressed at our daily departures. In most cases, a calm attitude on your part and a regular schedule will reduce his anxiety, but sometimes a gentle calming herbal treatment will work wonders.

- Try making a calming tea: 1 part valerian (tagar) and 1 part musta. Steep 1/2 a teaspoon in a cup of hot water for 5–10 minutes, cool and pour over the food.
- Almond milk: soak 10 raw almonds in water overnight. Peel the skins and put the almonds in the blender. Add a half cup of warm milk, a little ginger, a pinch of nutmeg and saffron. Good for dogs who can handle dairy.
- Massage the dog's scalp and feet (using a little of the proper oil for his dosha).

If these simple measures don't work, see your vet. There are various medications, which will not have to be used permanently, that can help your dog regain his equilibrium. .

Arthritis

Arthritis occurs when the joints wear down and stiffen. It can happen as a result of the aging process, but can also occur in response to trauma. When this happens, it can develop very fast – within a matter of weeks. Dogs with arthritis usually have obvious pain, stiffness, and slowed-down movements. They may be reluctant to climb stairs or exercise. Overweight dogs and large breeds are most at risk. The pulse will be thin and fast.

Vata-type Arthritis

- Vata pacifying diet. Feed warm, easy-to-digest foods. Avoid corn and potatoes.
- Give one tablet of Yogaraj Guggulu or Guggulu Rasayana (available commercially) once or twice a day.
- Ashwagandha or frankincense is helpful for Vata- and Kapha-type arthritis. It counters stress and acts as an anti-inflammatory.
- Gentle massage.
- Emerald is a good stone for Vata type arthritis.

Pitta-type Arthritis

- Pitta-pacifying diet.
- Ayurvedic herbal combination: kaishore guggulu (1/2 tablet) commercial formula twice a day; 1/4 teaspoon *sudarshan,* a commercial herbal formula whose main ingredient is the herb Chirayata *(Swertia chirataone)* a day.
- Emeralds or dark pearls are a good stone for Pitta type arthritis.
- An anti-arthritic diet that has helped many dogs is a combination of 2 parts brown rice, 2 parts barley pearls, 1 part lentils, 2 parts carrots, 1 cup celery, 1/2 cup parsley, 2 parts spinach, 2 parts lamb or beef heart, 2 garlic cloves, 10 parts water. Combine ingredients, bring to a boil, and simmer for an hour and a quarter. Feed for one month, twice a day.

Kapha-type Arthritis

In Kapha type, this disease is often due to an overbalance of Slesaka, a sub-dosha of the Kapha type.

- Kapha-reducing diet. No dairy products.
- Punarnava guggulu commercial formula (1/2 tablet) twice a day.

- Ashawagandha or boswellia (frankincense) for stress and as an anti-inflammatory. Give 10 drops of liquid ashwaganda for every ten pounds of body weight after meals, or one 500 mg tablet twice a day for dogs up to 60 pounds; give three times a day for larger dogs.
- For all types a beneficial color is yellow.
- Red coral is the traditional Ayurvedic gem for arthritis, but because of the danger to coral reefs worldwide, it can no longer be recommended.

Back Pain

This is a common problem in older dogs and dogs with basset, corgi, or dachshund conformation. Cage rest is usually critical. Serious problems such as herniated ("slipped") disk must be treated immediately by a qualified veterinarian.

- Herbs: Musta (1/4 teaspoon) twice a day. This relieves muscle spasms.
- Commercial formula: Yogaraj guggulu 2 times a day or kaishore guggulu once or twice a day.
- Massage with some mahanarayam oil. Kapha dogs usually need a deeper massage than Vata or Pitta types. Do not massage if you suspect disk or spine damage. Back massage is for muscular pain only.
- Decrease intake of Vata-producing foods.
- Avoid exposure to cold weather.
- Restrict exercise.
- Beneficial Color: Orange.

Bad Breath

Bad breath is not a disease in itself but a sign of another problem, usually, but not always in the mouth.

- Check the gums and teeth. Tartar, redness, and similar conditions suggest a problem. Take your dog for a professional cleaning, and then continue to care for your dog's teeth by regular brushing with canine toothpaste. You can also use a gentle Ayurvedic toothpaste containing neem or an herbal formula. The important thing is to brush your dog's teeth regularly.

Bladder Stones (Urolithiasis)

Bladder stones are common in dogs, and they can form almost the way an oyster makes pearls. The nidus, or center, of the stone is caused by something as tiny as a bacterium. Minerals are then deposited on the surface. There may be a single large deposit, or many smaller crystals. Signs include straining to urinate and blood in the urine; they can be identified by x-rays or ultra-sound.

Dogs can also get kidney stones, but less commonly. These are usually unrelated to bladder stones.

There are several types of bladder stones common in dogs:

- Struvite stones (magnesium ammonium phosphate or triple phosphate), or Kapha- type stones develop in an insufficiently acid environment. Specialty diets are available, but you can also provide such a diet at home: lower protein, lower magnesium, and lower phosphorus. Make sure the dog gets plenty of water. You are trying to lubricate and acidify the tract. Cranberry juice or tablets may also help. However, only use this diet if you know for sure that your dog has struvite stones. If he has oxalate stones (below) it can make the situation worse.
- Oxalate stones (Pitta-type) are most common in male dogs; these stones do not respond to dietary management. There is a substance called nephrocalcin in urine, which naturally inhibits the formation of oxalate stones. This substance is defective in dogs that form calcium oxalate bladder stones. The production of defective nephrocalcin may be a genetic problem. The stones form in an *acidic* environment (opposite to struvite stones). They can occur in dogs taking Lasix for heart problems. You may add oral potassium citrate (20-37.5mg/pound body weight) to help prevent further formation of the stones. Dogs who tend to form oxalate stones should never be fed potatoes or other food high in oxalic acid. After the stones have been removed avoid feeding dairy products, vitamin C supplements, or spinach (not that most dogs like spinach). Chocolate is full of oxalic acid as well, but chocolate is toxic to dogs in any case.
- Uric Acid stones (Vata-type): These stones develop in an over-acidic environment and are similar to gout in human beings, except that the stones accumulate in the bladder instead of the

joints. Dalmatians, an extremely Vata type breed, are genetically susceptible. This kind of stone may also indicate liver problems. The causative agent is purine, and dog's diagnosed with this disease should be on a low salt, low purine diet. Purine free foods include eggs and cheese (but not meat), and your vet can prescribe a commercial diet designed just for this purpose. Yeast and vitamin C supplements should be avoided in dogs diagnosed with uric acid stones. The Indian herb Pashana Bheda (*saxifrage ligulata* Wall) is considered the best Ayurvedic herb to dissolve uric acid stones. Dalmatians may have this kind of stone due to the lack of an important enzyme. They need special medication.

Surgical removal is the fastest and most direct way of getting rid of bladder stones. Small ones can sometimes be flushed out, but larger ones require a surgical incision. Dogs who tend to get bladder stones must be given as much water as they can drink and should be allowed to urinate frequently. Keeping these dogs in crates for any extended period (more than a couple of hours) can increase the chances of the stones re-forming. With any kind of bladder stone, keep your dog well hydrated.

Bleeding (External)

Apply a clean cloth and pressure to the site. Don't keep pulling off the cloth to see if the bleeding has stopped; you will only pull off the scab that is forming.

- Apply cold in the form of an icebag or bag of frozen vegetables.
- In minor cases, use a little aloe and turmeric powder mixed into a paste.
- Cool ash formed from burning a cotton ball will also help (the ball must be natural cotton, though, not a synthetic).
- Use a paste of astringent herbs such as lodbra, kushha, and bilva. You can use separately or combine them in equal proportions.
- Emerald, rubies, and blue sapphires may also be helpful.

Rectal bleeding may indicate a serious problem. Check with the veterinarian. A traditional remedy for rectal bleeding is a mixture of lobdra, kusththa or bilva. You can use separately or combine in equal proportions, two or three times a day. (See also ***Hematoma.***)

Bloat

This is a lethal condition in which the stomach fills with gas; it can then twist (gastric torsion) and cut off the blood supply to the vital organs. Dogs showing signs of bloat must immediately be taken to the emergency clinic for surgery. In Ayurvedic practice, bloat is a Vata disease, and occurs in Great Danes, Bloodhounds, St. Bernards, Basset Hounds, Gordon Setters, Pointers, and Weimaraners. To help prevent bloat, follow a Vata-reducing diet.

- Add Guggulu Rasayana (commercially available).
- Feed several smaller meals a day.
- Do not feed kibble only.
- Do not feed from a raised bowl – this allows too much Vata (air) to get into the system.

Every meal should include any product whose active ingredient is simethecone.

Bone Diseases

Proper treatment depends upon the precise diagnosis.

- Sapphire and rubies are excellent stones for most bone problems.

Burns

Flush the burned area with cool running water. Apply a moist dressing and bandage loosely. Make a 1/4 tablespoonful of sandalwood and turmeric paste and place in a tablespoonful of aloe vera gel directly to the burned area. Always take the dog to a vet for major burns.

Cancer

Cancer occurs when the DNA instructions for replication of certain cells go haywire. Sometimes the cause is damage to the DNA itself (from free radicals or radiation); other causes may be chemical carcinogens or even viruses. Normally cells can repair damaged DNA, but when they cannot, and when the immune system is unable to step in and get rid of the bad cells, cancer can develop.

In Ayurvedic theory cancer has a strong emotional component, often stemming from having no purpose in life. Perhaps the huge upswing we see in canine cancers (occurring at younger and younger ages) is the result of our companion animals feeling useless, drifting along from moment to moment with no sheep to herd, birds to hunt, or rabbits to kill. While most of us will not be returning to a pre-urban lifestyle, it's important to remember that dogs need things to do. Without a purpose they languish, suppress their life forces, and become ill.
Color: Green

Canine Cognitive Dysfunction

This is a geriatric disease very similar to Alzheimer's in people. In Kapha dogs, this problem is due to an overbalance of *Tarpaka,* a sub-dosha of Kapha. Give a Kapha- reducing diet. Carrots are also helping in aiding memory; sweet potatoes, okra, spinach and milk may also help.

Memory *(Medhya)* formula:

- Brhami, jatamansi, and bhringaraj can be sprinkled on the dog's food separately or mixed in equal proportions and made into a tea.
- Onyx is an excellent gem for dogs with this condition.

Cardiac Problems

In veterinary medicine the most commonly seen heart problems in dogs are congestive heart failure and cardiomyopathy (degeneration of the heart muscle). Signs of heart trouble include night and early morning coughing, shortness of breath, swelling in legs or abdomen, lethargy and increased sleep, and general weakness. Unfortunately, this problem is being seen at increasingly younger ages.

In Ayurvedic theory, the heart is the source of prana, ojas, and even mind. While dogs are not prone (as a rule) to high blood pressure and high cholesterol, heart failure is quite common, especially in older animals. Most heart disease in dogs is a result of an overbalance of *Sadhaka*, a sub-dosha of Pitta. The pulse will be swanlike. Give a Pitta-reducing diet and herbs. Avoid red meat and salt. Recommended herbs include aloe, arjuna, barberry, gotu kola, motherwort, myrrh, saffron, shatavari, sandalwood and katuka.

For Vata-type heart disease, give an anti-Vata diet (warm, heavy, moist foods) and herbs such as ashwagandha, arjuna, astragalus, cinnamon, cardamom, comfrey root, ginseng, guggul, licorice and sandalwood.

For Kapha-type heart disease, avoid giving your dog sugar, dairy, cheese, butter, eggs, fatty meats, lard and salt. Keep consumption of vitamin/mineral supplements to a minimum. The B vitamins may be taken. However, avoid vitamins A, D and E. Give herbs that encourage the breakup of phlegm. Other helpful herbs include bayberry, cayenne, cinnamon, arjuna, calamus, and cardamom. Arjuna preparations and Trikatu with honey are herbal combinations often prescribed. Avoid licorice.

Gem for Kapha type heart disease: ruby or garnet.

Chanting of AUM is considered helpful to open the channels.

Herbs to improve heart function:

- Arjuna. This is the primary Indian heart herb. Give 1/4 teaspoon 2 or 3 times a day in a little honey and warm water. Arjuna is a coronary vasodilator. Note: the western herb hawthorn has basically the same benefits are Arjuna.
- Ginger. Add some grated ginger to your dog's food.
- Garlic. Add a bit of garlic to the dog's food.
- Combine 4 parts punarnava, 2 parts kutki, -1/4 part gulwel sattva, and 1/4 part shilajit. Steep 1/2 teaspoon in a cup of warm water, and pour over food once or twice a day.
- Guggul, Bala, Manjista are also used with good effect by some Ayurvedic practitioners.
- Rudraksha, also known as the "tears of Shiva," are considered good for the heart. You can soak a couple of the dried seeds in water overnight and then give the water to the dog.
- Vitamin therapy: Consider adding co-enzyme Q10, a fat-soluble vitamin-like substance to your dog's diet. Q10 helps produce needed energy in all cells, and has been found to be particularly beneficial to hearts.
- The amino acid L-carnitine has also been found to be helpful.

Color: Green

Cataracts

Cataracts are considered a Kapha disorder.
Prevention: Prevention is important, and traditional prevention eyewash consists of a Triphala tea eyewash. Boil 1 teaspoon of Triphala in a cup of water for a couple of minutes. Cool, and carefully strain through cheesecloth. Wash the eye carefully twice a day.
Herbal: You can also use this internal tea: 5 parts punarnava, 3 parts shatavari, and three parts brahmi. Give 1/4 teaspoon twice a day to help prevent cataracts.
Supplement: Some people have had good luck supplementing a cataract-developing dog's diet with co-enzyme Q10 (15–30 mg), depending on the size of the dog. This may be used with other antioxidants.
Gem: Jade

Circulation

In Vata dogs, circularity problems are usually caused by an overbalance of the Vyana sub-dosha. A Vata-reducing diet and herbal therapy may be in order.

Colitis

Colitis is a very general term and can refer to any one of a number of diseases of the intestinal tract, generally in the colon (large intestine). Examples are acute colitis, inflammatory bowel disease, irritable bowel syndrome, and others. Causes can include parasites (especially whipworms), bacteria, foreign bodies, polyps, cancer, and many more. See your vet if the disease does not respond to simple home remedies.

Basic colon health can often be maintained by regular consumption of the Triphala combination, available commercially.

In Ayurvedic theory, colitis occurs when Vata pushes Pitta into the colon, causing inflammation. Treatment consists in pacifying Pitta.

- Herbal remedy: 4 parts shatavari, 1/8 part shanka bhamsa, 1/8 part kama dudba, and 2 parts sanjivani.

- Add a peeled, cooked, seeded, pulped apple or a little apple juice to your dog's food with just a pinch of nutmeg. The point is to increase fiber.

Conjunctivitis

The conjunctiva, the tissue coating the eye and lining the eyelids, serves as a protective barrier for the eye. Problems in this area can be caused by viral or bacterial infection, corneal disease, allergies, trauma or other problems. If simple home treatment does not clear the condition up, see your vet.

Signs include red eyes, often with discharge, light sensitivity, squinting, or pawing at the eye.

In Ayurvedic theory, conjunctivitis is a Pitta condition. While most likely to occur in Pitta-type dogs, it can appear any time in which there is an excess of Pitta.

- Flush the eye with a sterile solution.
- Coriander eyelid wash: Steep 1 teaspoon of coriander leavers in a cup of boiling water for 15 minutes or so. Strain, cool and place over the dog's closed eyelids.
- Cilantro eyelid wash: Make a pulp of fresh cilantro leaves and blend into 1/4 cup of water. Apply to the closed eyelids. You can also feed it to your dog.
- Make a goat's milk compress using sterilized cotton balls.
- Make a tea of 1 part kama dydha and 1 part gulwel sattva. Put half a teaspoon in water and pour over the food once or twice a day for a week.
- Wipe the eyes with a turmeric solution. Stir some turmeric into pure water. Place a clean cloth in the liquid, and then let it dry. You can use the cloth to wipe the eye clean. (The cloth will turn yellow.)
- For an antibiotic effect, mix 1 part turmeric, 1 part neem, and 1 part manjisthra. Give 1/4 teaspoon twice a day with meals.
- Pitta-type dogs benefit from a Triphala eyewash. Boil 1 teaspoon of Triphala in a cup for three minutes. Cool and strain *completely,* so that no particles are left. Wash the eye gently.

Constipation

Constipation is not as common in dogs as it is in people, and the problem is often attributable to being fed bones, especially pork bones, which can form a terrible impaction. Older dogs are most at risk, but younger ones who have eaten something they shouldn't have may also be victims. However, what many people mistake for constipation could be an intestinal block, a very serious condition. It could also be due to blocked or abscessed anal sacs. Your vet should see a dog that has constipation for more than a day.

Dogs with true constipation pass dry hard stools; they may also have flatulence and discomfort. The pulse will be a strong frog pulse. Most cases of constipation are caused by too little fiber in the diet, too little water, and too little exercise. In Ayurveda tradition, the way to get rid of constipation is to pacify Vata by following a Vata-reducing diet.

- Add -1/2 teaspoon of the Ayurvedic herbal combination Triphala to a cup of hot water; let it stand for several minutes. Then add to the meal.
- Add fiber such as wheat bran, Metamucil, baby green beans, or canned pumpkin to the meal.
- Add flaxseed oil to the diet.
- Supplement with brewer's yeast
- Add water to the food.
- Add a vegetable enzyme to the food.
- Increase exercise.
- Guggulu Rasayana (available commercially), give 1/2 teaspoon once a day.

Coughing (see also Kennel Cough and Flu)

It's important to note what kind of cough the dog has. A dry Vata cough is treated differently from a productive Kapha cough or one with a greenish or yellow mucous (Pitta cough) that may signal infection. Coughs can be a sign not only of a respiratory infection, but also of heartworm or other heart damage. It's important to treat the underlying

> *Dry coughs often suggest an overbalance in the* Prana *sub-dosha of Vata.*

condition at the same time as the cough. Dry coughs do best with a cough suppressant, but a productive cough and coughs due to infection should be treated with expectorants.

Herbs and Teas:

- In traditional Ayurvedic medicine a dry cough is treated with a tea made from half a teaspoon of *talisadi* and a half a teaspoon of licorice with a bit of honey poured over the food.
- A productive cough is treated with a combination of 1/4 teaspoon of black pepper with 1 teaspoon of honey. Or a tea can be made from 1/2 a tablespoon of ginger powder, a pinch of clove and little cinnamon. Stubborn coughs may benefit from mixing 1/2 teaspoon of ground mustard and 1/2 a teaspoon of ginger powder or clove with honey two or three times a day.
- For a cough resulting from infection, be sure that the infection is also treated. You can then make a tea with 1/4 teaspoon each of sitopaladi and maha sudarshan. Give three times a day with honey.
- Mullein rasayana, available commercially; one teaspoon in hot water once a day.

The following herbs support the bronchi and can be used in cases of cough: mullein, licorice, cinnamon, tulasi, bayberry, yerba sante, ajwan, shilajit, pippali, amalaki, bhibitaki, flax seed, Irish moss, turmeric, ginger, fenugreek, cardamom, cubeb, clove, black pepper, myrrh.

Beneficial Color: Yellow

Cystitis

The word cystitis means an inflammation of the bladder. It is a very general term and can apply to a variety of ailments. It is usually applied to any disease that irritates the urinary tract. In dogs, the most common cause of cystitis is a bacterial infection. However, the problem can also be bladder stones, tumors, or polyps in the bladder. The most common sign is blood in the urine. Some dogs may also show discomfort while urinating or only pass a small amount of urine at a time. Your vet will need to perform a urinalysis, urine culture, and perhaps take x-rays to determine the precise cause. Bladder infections are treated with antibiotics. Some bladder stones can be addressed by dietary changes; others may require surgery.

In Vata dogs, the problem is likely to be an overbalance of *Apana,* a sub-dosha of Vata.

- Teas from coriander, cumin, or fennel may bring some relief, in addition to standard care. You can also make a tea from equal portions of these herbs.
- Mix 5 parts punanava, 4 parts gokshura, and 3 parts musta. Add 1/2 teaspoon to a half cup of warm water and give twice daily.

Dental Disease (Danta Roga)

Ayurvedic practitioners have been recommending tooth and tongue cleaning in India long before people in the west ever heard of a toothbrush! And while dogs are not prone to getting cavities (not enough sugar in their natural diet) they can develop calculus (calcium deposits) and gingivitis just as people can. The answer is to brush your dog's teeth regularly with canine toothpaste. Don't use toothpaste made for people (they're not designed to be swallowed). While your regular veterinarian can perform routine work such as cleaning and extractions, there are also real dog "dentists" who can do it all – root canals, tooth restorations, and – yup – braces.

Herbal: Akarkara. It relieves pain and permits the free flow of saliva.

Depression

See Lethargy.

Diabetes Mellitus

Diabetes mellitus is a serious metabolic illness that occurs when insufficient insulin is being produced. You will need to monitor your dog's glucose. (The normal range for blood glucose in dogs is around 60 to 110 mg/dL or 3.9 to 6.1 mmol/L.) The pulse will have a knotty, thin feel to it.

Diabetic dogs need regular veterinary care, a controlled diet, and almost always insulin. Diet changes alone are not enough to control diabetes in dogs, although it works occasionally in people.

However, feeding the proper diet may somewhat reduce the need for insulin and keep the dog on a more "even keel" so that blood sugar (glucose) doesn't go shooting up and down. In Ayurvedic theory, diabetes is a Kapha disorder, where the digestive fire (agni) is diminished. This leads to high blood sugar. The following mixtures may be helpful in maintain correct blood sugar.

Another rarer form, diabetes inspidus, occurs when the kidney is insensitive to ADH (the anti-diuretic hormone).

- Herbs and diet
  - o Follow a Kapha-pacifying diet –limiting your dog's intake of sweets, carbohydrates, and dairy products. Your vet can provide a specific diet for your particular dog.
  - o Increase bitter and pungent foods.
  - o 1 part guduchi, 1 part sharunika, 1 part kutki, and 2 parts punarnava. Give 1/4 teaspoon twice a day with food and warm water.
  - o Give a 1/4 teaspoon of turmeric 2 twice a day.
  - o Gudmar and Shilajit herbs may be helpful.
  - o Put a cup of water in a copper bowl overnight, and give to the dog in the morning.
- Try *Abhyanga* massage.
- Gems: Coral and emerald.
- Color: Yellow

Diarrhea

Diarrhea is not a disease in itself, but usually a sign of another condition. In dogs, whose owners don't pay enough attention to their pet's dosha, it usually occurs as a result of eating spoiled or otherwise unsuitable food. Dogs evolved to be scavengers, so they have a tendency to grab anything within reach. Most cases of diarrhea are not serious in dogs, although it can be quite dangerous in puppies, which have little reserves. That is one reason why parvovirus is so deadly in puppies, but comparatively mild in adults. Most cases of diarrhea resolve themselves. Make sure your dog has plenty of fresh water to drink, but feed only very lightly – just enough to give him the items suggested below. You want to give the digestive tract a "rest."

If the diarrhea continues for more than two days, or if it is bloody or very smelly, take your dog to the vet. Causes can include viral infection or bacterial infection, colitis, worms, food allergy, and many other diseases. Diarrhea can occur in dogs that are on a course of antibiotics, as these medications destroy the good bacteria as well as the bad.

In Ayurvedic terms, diarrhea occurs when Agni, the digestive fire, is weak. The general plan is to strengthen the Agni and pacify whatever Vata condition is causing the diarrhea. This is usually Pitta, so it's best to put the dog on a Pitta-reducing diet first.

It's best to fast the dog for 12 hours, although you should continue to give water. You may add the following, however:

- Add well-cooked apples (or applesauce) or canned pumpkin to a little food, with 1/2 teaspoon of ghee, and a little nutmeg and cardamom. You can also try adding a little mashed banana. These foods have plenty of fiber. A particularly good source of pure fiber is pectin, which you can buy at health food store. Mix the pectin into the food well – don't sprinkle it on the top.
- Add cooked rice (1/2 cup), 2 tablespoons yogurt, and 1/2 tablespoon of ghee.
- Mix 1/4 teaspoon of ginger powder with 1/2 teaspoon of sugar. Give twice a day for a day or so.
- Add 1/4 teaspoon fennel powder with 1/4 teaspoon of ginger powder. Add to the food twice a day for a few days.
- If the diarrhea is a result of antibiotic treatment, add probiotics to his food twice a day, available at any health food store. Continue the dosage for at least two weeks after the antibiotic treatment is finished. A month or two is even better.

Ear Infection and Inflammation

Ear infections are very common in dogs, especially those with floppy ears such as cocker spaniels and basset hounds. All too often we see a continual round of antibiotic treatment, followed by brief periods of "clearing up" before the infection returns. Chronic ear infections suggest allergies or other immune problem, or even a heart or liver disorder. Even when the problem is solely in the ear, this extremely painful condition deserves immediate attention. Ear infections are often due to a combination of fungal and antibiotic agents, and both should be treated. Some extremely tough bacteria, such as pseudomonas, have become extremely resistant to antibiotics, which must be given early and aggressively if the infection is to be controlled.

To help prevent ear infection, clean your dog's ears regularly with a gentle, non-alcohol cleaner. Many good commercial products are available. Vinegar is also very good. Dry the ear carefully afterwards.

Infected ears are often red and smelly, and the dog will scratch at them. In very mild cases you can clean the ear with a combination of tea tree oil and neem. (Neem is a powerful antifungal and antiparasitic.) Both substances must be well diluted. Add about 10 drops of tea tree oil and ten drops of neem to an ounce of sesame oil. Apply gently to the ear canal.

Antibiotic herbal treatment:

1 part turmeric, 1 part goldenseal, 1 part echinacea. (Be sure to use commercial, organically grown goldenseal. This plant is so beneficial that it has been hunted almost to extinction. Use 1/2 teaspoon in hot water and add to the dog's food twice a day for a week. If the ear infection does not clear up, see your vet. These can be painful and serious. If the infection is not brought under control, expensive surgery might be necessary.)Oil of mullein is a western herb that also works well. Follow the instructions on the label.
Gem: Yellow sapphire.

Eye Problems (also see specific problem)

Eye problems can be very hard for owners to evaluate and special equipment is usually needed. If you suspect an eye problem, consult a vet right away; your dog's eyesight may be at stake. Eye problems include conjunctivitis, dry eye, abscess, edema, cataracts, brain tumor, retinal degeneration, cherry eye, glaucoma, proptosed globe (eye proptosis), corneal ulcer, allergic reaction and other conditions.

Many eye problems, especially if they occur along with problems in the ear and throat, are due to overbalance of the *Udana*, a sub-dosha of Vata. Impairment of vision can be due to an

overbalance of *Alochaka,* a sub-dosha of Pitta. The pulse will be hard, slow, and "slippery."
Gems: lapis lazuli, coral, and opal.

Flatulence

Flatulence and gas is a smelly and annoying (but not usually serious) condition. However, it should be noted that many dogs prone to flatulence are also candidates for bloat, which can be deadly.

In Ayurvedic theory, flatulence builds up from excess Vata in the colon.

- Add a charcoal tablet to meals to absorb the gases.
- Add simethecone (available in many commercial products; however, be sure not to buy something with "extra" active ingredients.
- Give a Vata-pacifying diet.
- Give a Triphala herbal compound. Take 1/2 a teaspoon of the Triphala mixture and add it to a cup of boiling water for 5 minutes.
- For gassy spells, try adding a commercial tablet containing shankavati and lasundivati for a few days.

Glaucoma

Glaucoma is a condition in which the intraocular pressure of the eye rises to very high levels. In Ayurvedic theory, it is due to an accumulation of Kapha, and Kapha dogs like Basset Hounds are most at risk.

Primary glaucoma (that is, glaucoma that is not a result of something else) comes in two major types: closed angle and open angle. Open angle glaucoma is the kind people and beagles tend to get. Closed angle glaucoma is also found in other dog breeds and is a serious and painful condition, almost inevitably leading to blindness. Blindness in dogs is not the tragedy that is can be to people, however. With their superexcellent sense of smell, dogs usually manage to live a comfortable and happy life. They can still smell their dinners, and that's the most important thing. To help prevent glaucoma in breeds with a predilection toward these conditions, such as bassets, try to prevent eye pressure buildup.

The easiest way to do this is to avoid collars, and choose a harness instead. Studies show that even a slight tug on a collar can start the process of glaucoma. Prevention measures also include:

- Herbal tea: 5 parts punarnava, 3 parts jatamansi, and 3 parts shanka pushpin. Boil 1 teaspoon of the mix in a cup of water and give one or twice a day mixed with food.
- Avoid over-exercise.
- Kapha reducing diet.
- Triphala eyewash: Boil 1/2 teaspoon of Triphala in a cup of water. Strain exceedingly well so that no particles remain in the wash and bathe the eye with the cool tea. When glaucoma appears suddenly, it is an extreme veterinary emergency. Do not delay in taking your dog to the animal hospital.

Hearing Loss

In Ayurveda, hearing loss is governed by a weakening of *Prana,* a sub-dosha of Vata; it occurs most commonly in older dogs. The pulse will feel quick and widening. While most hearing loss is irreversible, a couple of Ayurvedic treatments may help:

- Yogaraj gugguli is a commercial tablet that pacifies Vata. Give 100 mg of the compound twice daily.
- Feed a Vata-pacifying diet.
- Try putting a little garlic oil to ear. Squeeze a few drops of garlic into a tablespoon of warm sesame oil and massage it into the ear. Do not use oil if any infection is present in the ear.

Heart Problems (See Cardiac Problems)

Hematoma

A hematoma is a blood-filled swelling, and is common on the ears of hunting dogs.

- Make a paste of 1 teaspoon of turmeric powder, 1 teaspoon of sandalwood powder, and a pinch of alum. Mix with enough water to form a paste and apply.

Hemorrhagic Gastroenteritis (HGE)

This life-threatening, but non-contagious condition has no known cause. It simply shows up, usually in small dogs. It is characterized by a great deal of bloody, foul-smelling diarrhea and is often accompanied by vomiting. Affected dogs need to be given large amount of IV fluids immediately and antibiotics. Untreated animals usually die. If you suspect this disease, have your dog treated by a qualified vet immediately. The recovering dog can be treated for diarrhea, above.

Incoordination

Incoordination is most clearly indicated by a wobbling as the dog walks. His feet may cross over each other, but he may seem unaware of it. Technically, this condition is known as lack of proprioception. Causes can include spinal cord tumors, spinal disc disease, brain tumor, poisoning, middle or inner ear disease, and a host of other problems. The cause must be identified before treatment can begin.

Infections

Infections include both bacterial and viral diseases. They can be exacerbated by stress, a bad diet, or toxins in the environment. However, we should not overlook the major importance genetics plays. Just as in people, some well cared for, wellfed dogs simply "catch everything," while others – who seem in poor condition and subsist on a bad diet, seem immune to all those little bugs.
Herbs: There are a great many Ayurvedic and western herbs such as Echinacea that help boost immunity. Choose one suited for your dog's dosha, and follow the instructions.
Vitamins: Dogs with persistent infections may do well with a supplement of multi-vitamins.
Beneficial Color: Orange and yellow.

Insect Bites and Stings

In Ayurvedic terms, a sting or bite produces an aggravation of Pitta under the skin. Most of the time, the sting is only painful;

however, some dogs can experience anaphylactic reaction, which can result in breathing interruption and even death. If your dog seems to have a hard time catching his breath after a sting, take him to your veterinarian immediately. As he is recovering,

- Apply a paste of equal parts sandalwood and turmeric (add sufficient water to make a paste).
- Herbalized neem paste or oil (do not use the pure extract) may be beneficial.
- Apply diluted neem and/or tea tree oil to the spot.

There are more exotic remedies, such as burning some dried coconut and applying the ash (which contains antihistamines), but keeping neem paste on hand is quicker.

Fleas and ticks are the most common external irritants of dogs. Many dogs are allergic to flea bites, while ticks carry a multitude of diseases. Keep your dog on a commercial, prescription *flea and tick program. These are very safe and effective.*

Irritable Bowel Syndrome (IBS)

This is a common problem in dogs, and can be caused by food intolerances, allergies, bacteria, or even parasites. It's most typical sign is diarrhea, although some animals may also vomit. In Ayurvedic theory, IBS can occur when Vata pushes Pitta into the colon. Balancing herbal treatments includes:

- 2 parts arrowroot, 1 part shatavari, 1/8 part kama dudha, and 1/8 part shanka bhasma. Give 1/4 teaspoon twice a day in the food.
- 1/2 teaspoon of sat isabgol (psylloum husks) in a 1/4 cup of yogurt.
- Triphala. For dogs up to 30 pounds give 1/2 tablet twice daily, dogs from 30-60 pounds 1 tablet twice daily, and 1 1/2 tablets twice daily for larger dogs.
- Boswellia: Dogs up to 30 pounds, one 500 mg capsule twice daily, dogs up to 60 pounds, 1 capsule three times daily; larger dogs 2 capsules twice daily.
- Boil 1/2 teaspoon of flaxseed in half a cup of water and feed during the evening meal.

Kennel Cough and Flu (see also Coughs)

While dogs don't get ordinary colds, they are susceptible to the highly contagious kennel cough and its more serious, recent-appearing relative, canine influenza. There's no real cure for these viral diseases, only supportive care. In Ayurveda theory, these conditions are considered a Kapha-Vata disorder. The standard Ayurvedic remedy for cold and flulike symptoms is ginger.

- The classic recipe is a mix of 1 part ginger, 1 part cinnamon, and 2 parts lemongrass. Steep a teaspoon for ten minute in hot water, strain (add honey if you want) and pour it over the food.
- Mix 4 teaspoons of fennel seed powder with half a teaspoon of sugar and add to the food twice a day.
- Mix 1/4 teaspoon cinnamon with 1/2 teaspoon of honey. Give twice a day.
- Make a tea of the Indian herb *tulsi* (holy basil) in a cup of water. Pour over the food.
- Add a supplement of vitamin C.
- Do not feed dairy products to dogs with coughs or flu-like signs.
- Do not over-exercise the dog.

Beneficial Color: Yellow.
Aromas: Cinnamon, ajwan, tumeric, ginger, cardamon, clove, or myrrh.

Hair Loss

Hair loss in dogs is usually a sign of another problem, unless of course you own a Chinese Crested or American Hairless Terrier! Sometimes, the cause is a local irritation or injury – flea bite, hot spot, and so on. Sometimes it can signal a more subtle metabolic problem like Addison's or Cushing's disease. The following oils may help hair growth, but it is important to discover and deal with the causative agent.

- Massage the bald spot with a little brahmi or bhringaraj oil. You can also try some vitamin E oil. The oil helps, and the massage helps – so both together "double-team" the bald spot.
- Add more cheese and yogurt to the diet.
- Add other food high in calcium, magnesium and zinc.

- Shampoo with a mixture of the following herbs: 5 parts dashamoola, 4 parts bhringaraj, and 3 parts jatamamsi. Add 1/2 a teaspoon of the herbal mixture to whole milk or cream and heat. Cool and use as a nourishing rinse after a shampoo. Let the mixture stay on for ten minutes before rinsing thoroughly.

Dogs who lose hair may be stressed. Take equal portions of jatamamsi and brahmi and steep a teaspoonful of the mixture in a cup of hot water. Cool and pour over the dog's food.

Kidney Problems (See also Bladder Stones)

Kidney disease is quite common in older dogs, and usually involves chronic inflammation and formation of scar tissue. Signs include excessive thirst and urination, weight loss, vomiting, poor coat, and in later stages, a smell of urine on the skin and mouth.

In Ayurvedic theory most kidney problems are caused by high Pitta, which can manifest itself as crystals in the urine, or even by kidney or bladder stones.

Herbal:

- Mix equal parts punarnava, fennel seed, and gokshura and give 1/2 a teaspoon twice a day with meals. Although Punarnava can raise Pitta, nevertheless it *is* recommended for this special case.
- Make a tea of 1/4 teaspoon each of cumin, coriander, and fennel by mixing equal amounts and boiling. Give the cooled teas twice a day.
- Mix 1/2 teaspoon musta with 1/2 teaspoon fennel, steep for ten minutes in hot water, strain, and give once a day.
- Gokshura *(Tribulus terrestris),* a mild diuretic herb.
- Diet: Your vet may recommend a low-protein diet for dogs with kidney disease.
- The western herb dandelion is also a superior diuretic and may be used with great effect.

Gem: Jade

Beneficial Color: Yellow

Lameness

Lameness is yet another condition with a wide variety of causes – everything from traumas like sprain (or even a thorn in the paw pad) to fever and swollen joints, cervical lesions, bone tumors, developmental bone disease, toe problems, hip dysplasia, arthritis, luxating patella, ruptured ACL (anterior cruciate ligament) and panosteitis (bone disease). If the cause is not immediately obvious – sore pads, a torn nail, or a cut – it's best to let your vet have a look at the dog. X-rays may be required.

In most cases of lameness, especially those involving ligaments, rest is essential. In some cases surgery is required. (A sprain is technically a disruption of a ligament or tendon. A ruptured cranial cruciate ligament is very common is young, active dogs.) Diagnosis usually includes a physical exam and x-ray. Treatment depends on the severity of the injury, and always involves a great deal of rest, as recovery is slow, taking up to 20 weeks for full recovery.

Herbal:

Several commercial Ayurvedic products are available.

- Murivenna: A cooling oil containing aloe vera in a coconut base, specific for sprains, inflammations, pain, wounds and joint discomforts. Specific ingredients may include coconut oil, aloe, Indian coral tree, horseradish tree, borreria, Indian beech, betel pepper, garlic, and wild asparagus.
- Siddha Kayathirumeni Thailam (cooling oil).
- Siddha Kayathirumeni Enna (oil).
- Give 1/4 teaspoon of turmeric powder with warm water twice a day.
- Yogarajagulgulu (pill).

Leaky Bladder (Bladder Atonia)

This is a frequent problem is spayed females, in which the bladder sphincter muscles become weak. Younger dogs will sometimes heal on their own, but older dogs may need regular treatment. Your veterinarian has mainstream medication that will help, but you can also try this ancient Ayurvedic formula:

- A tablespoon of crushed white sesame seeds, half a teaspoon of brown sugar, and some water. Give once or twice a day.

Lethargy

Lethargy can be a sign of mental depression or a physical illness. If your formerly active dog suddenly shows no interest in play or food, or seems unresponsive to you, it may be a sign of another condition. While Ayurveda has some answers for a simple case of low-energy or the blahs, it's important to know whether or not something more serious is occurring, such as heart failure, muscle disease, arthritis, bone tumors, spinal disease, kidney failure, infection or a host of other diseases associated with this behavior.

In Kapha dogs, lethargy may be due to an overbalance of *Avalambaka,* a sub-dosha of Kapha. Give a Kapha-reducing diet. The lethargy may also be due to another condition, however, that should be treated first.
Beneficial Color: Red

Liver Problems

The liver is the largest gland in the body, and one of the most critical, for it is the body's major detoxifier. Liver problems are most common in older dogs. Signs of liver trouble include vomiting, tiring, depression, swollen abdomen and irritability. The Ayurvedic pulse will be weak and splitting.
Herbs: Amla, bhringaraj, kutki. There is also a commercial product called Lvit-2 available in both liquid and tablet form. The formula contains multiple herbs, including kutki and amla. This is an excellent choice when the dog exhibits elevated liver enzymes. Give small dogs 10 drops of the medicine for every ten pounds of body weight twice daily. Dogs up to 60 pounds should have 1 tablet twice a day, and very large dogs should take the medicine three times a day for three months.
Beneficial Color: Blue or yellow

Mammary Gland Abnormalities

Dogs are well endowed by nature – with ten nipples. If you have a female dog with lumpy nipples, it might be that she is experiencing a false pregnancy (or a real one, if she is not spayed!) Or it could be mastitis, a bacterial infection of the gland, or tumors. Get an opinion from your vet.

Nuclear (Lenticular) Sclerosis

This is a common condition seen in an aging dog in which there is cloudiness in the lenses. On the surface, it looks like cataracts, but is much less serious, and does not significantly impair a dog's vision.

Oral Problems

If you are a faithful tooth-brusher, you will probably catch mouth problems before they become too serious. Sometimes smelling a dog's breath can give a clue as to an underlying problem: a dog with advanced kidney disease may have a urine-like breath, while an unusually sweet-mouthed dog may have diabetes. Broken or abscessed teeth are the most common mouth problem, particularly in dogs who don't get adequate dental care. However, oral tumors or even a foreign body caught in the teeth can also be possible.

Poisoning

Because dogs are so eager to eat they are easy to poison. They can be poisoned by all sorts of thing that no one in their right mind would eat, as well as by things that are safe for people but not for dogs. Common poisons include antidepressant drugs, flea and tick collars, antifreeze, fabric softeners, aspirin and ibuprofen, bleach, chocolate, caffeine, lead products (batteries), onions, petroleum distillates, and rat poison. If you suspect poisoning, contact your vet or the ASPCA Animal Poison Control Center at 1-888-4-Ani-help. Have your credit card ready.

Pyometra

Pyometra is a uterine infection, usually occurring in older unspayed animals. Signs include bloody or excessively mucoid discharge. Treatment is complex and not always successful, and the best treatment is immediate surgery. Without it your dog could die.

Rectal Problems

Swelling, redness, or itchiness in the rectal area are indicative of several problems including an impacted/infected/abscessed anal sac, perianal adenoma, tumor, perineal hernia, tapeworms, or even a behavioral problem. As in all good medicine, the treatment depends upon the cause.

Respiratory Problems

Respiratory problems include conditions that cause labored breathing and coughing. Any dog experiencing these problems should be rested until the cause of the condition can be discovered and treated. Possible causes include heart failure, anemia, fluid or blood in the lungs, pleural effusion, pneumonia, kennel cough, chronic bronchitis, and obstruction of the larynx.
Herbs: Ginger, Holy Basil (tulsi), Sitopaladi, Trikatu
Beneficial Colors: Orange or green

Reverse Sneezing

This is a problem that doesn't occur in people, who often find it rather distressing to hear in their dogs. The dog seems to be snorting or gagging. The cause is usually some irritation in the pharynx, often an allergy or sore throat. However, bad as it sounds (and it can go on for 30 seconds or so) most dogs don't seem unduly bothered by a reverse sneezing episode. Feeding your dog a soft food rather that dry irritating kibble may help. In more serious cases, the vet will prescribe antibiotics or an anti-inflammatory.
Color: Blue

Skin Problems

Skin problems come in many guises: lumps, infections, rashes, itches, sores, color changes, and others. Causes can range from simple shedding to hypothyroidism, Cushing's disease, mange, cysts, sebaceous gland adenoma, bacterial infection, ringworm, or lick granuloma. Other causes of skin problems include allergies (dust, pollen) and toxins in the environment.

While skin disorders are quite common in dogs, many can be cured or greatly alleviated simply by giving a better diet (higher quality, meat-based protein), supplemented with vitamins and minerals.

According to Ayurvedic tradition, many skin problems are due to an overbalance of *Bhrajaka,* a sub-dosha of Pitta.

Diet: Pitta reducing diet.

Herbal: An excellent commercial Ayurvedic compound called Neem Plus contains neem, amla, bahera, ahritaki (which three combine to make Triphala). Give small dogs 10 drops per ten pounds of body weight twice daily; dogs up to 30 pounds, 1 tablespoon twice daily; dogs up to 60 pounds, 1 tablet thrice daily, and very large dogs, 2 tablets twice daily. Neem shampoo or oil may be effective against ringworm, which is a fungus, and not a worm.

Color: Yellow

Gems: White or pink coral, yellow sapphire.

Straining

Dogs who are straining to move their bowels may have simple constipation. However, the cause is more likely colitis; if the resulting stool is mucoid, it's probably colitis. If it is hard and dry, it is constipation. It is also possible there is a foreign body in the intestinal tract, a tumor, a perineal hernia, or an anal sac abscess. Treatment depends upon the cause.

Thirst, Increased

A dog who beings drinking excessively may be suffering form any one of a number of diseases including diabetes, Cushing's disease, liver or kidney problems, pyometra, or be responding to the drug cortisone. In a few cases, the cause can be behavioral. Treatment depends on the cause.

Thyroid Problems

Hypothyroidism is quite common in older dogs. Here the thyroid is underactive, producing too little thyroid hormone. The pulse will be slow and wide. Many cases are mild or borderline, with no specific signs other than fatigue and depression. More serious deficiencies may first appear as a rough, sparse haircoat, with symmetrical hair loss. Your vet can provide inexpensive thyroid replacement tablets. It is also helpful for you to use Ayurvedic treatment to help speed up the metabolism. Useful herbs include jatamansi and Brahmi guggulu and shilajita.

Toenail Trouble

Dogs have a rather surprising amount of problems with their toenails – usually because they are cut too short or not short enough, but also because of possible bacterial or fungal infections, as well as immune mediated difficulties. A broken toenail can cause lameness. And yes, dogs can get ingrown toenails.

Urinary Incontinence

In normal dogs, a band of muscular tissue called the urethral sphincter, located at the base of the bladder, keeps urine from leaking. (It's essentially a valve.) Like people, dogs can consciously open and close the valve, but sometimes things go awry. In some cases the cause is behavioral. True incontinence is quite different from inappropriate elimination. Submissive urination is a tactic used by wild dogs to show dominant dogs that they respect their leadership. Unfortunately, humans don't react the same way to such displays, to the confusion and discouragement of the dog. However, other physical causes may also be at work. Most commonly, when incontinence shows up in older dogs, it is the spayed female who is the most likely victim, although very old males may also be affected. Medical treatment is available. Other causes may include an inherited condition called ectopic ureter (appearing in Siberian Huskies, Poodles, Labrador Retrievers, and other breeds). This condition can be corrected by surgery. An enlarged or inflamed bladder may also the villain. In any case, it's wise to check with your vet, who can perform numerous tests.

In Ayurveda, urinary incontinence is considered a Vata condition which asserts itself primarily in older dogs. (We are not talking here about housetraining problems, but true incontinence.) The following herbal mixture may help:

- Mix 5 parts ashwagandha with 3 parts bala and 2 parts vidari. Give -1/4 teaspoon twice a day with meals.
- Give a Vata-pacifying diet.

In Ayurveda, two commonly used herbs for this condition, *Crateva* and *Equisetum,* have been shown to be effective for human beings.

Acupressure on appropriate points may also prove helpful.

Urinary Tract Infection (See Cystitis)

Urination Abnormalities

Many conditions can results in abnormal urine. Bloody urine may indicate a bladder infection, bleeding disorder, or bladder stones. If a male dog is straining to urinate, suspect a urinary tract obstruction. Females who leak urine may have an estrogen deficiency. See "leaky bladder." Very dark urine may indicate liver disease or hemolytic anemia.

Vomiting

Vomiting is one of the most common signs of illness. Because dogs eat fast and worry about what they ate later, it's a good strategy for staying alive and un-poisoned. It can indicate roundworms, intestinal obstruction, bloat, gastric tumors, pancreatitis, food allergies, inflammatory bowel disease, and a dozen other conditions, some serious some not. Vomiting accompanied by obvious distress, diarrhea (especially bloody diarrhea) should be considered an emergency.

Wounds and Abscesses

Abscessed wounds often result in an agitated pulse.

An Ayurvedic commercial product called Phytogel is extremely effective for healing wounds. It is derived from Himalayan cedarwood oil. It has the added advantage that most dogs will not attempt to lick it off.

Beneficial Color: Green

Glossary

Adrak: Fresh ginger.

Agni: Digestive fire. It transforms food into energy.

Ahamkara: The concept of the individual "I" or ego.

Akarkara: An Ayurvedic herb.

Akasha: Space, the void.

Alochaka: A type of Pitta governing vision.

Alterative: Also known as "blood cleansers." These herbs improve lymphatic circulation, remove metabolic toxins, increase immunity, help clear chronic skin conditions, heal wounds, and reduce fevers. They also help detoxify the liver, kidneys, lungs, and colon. Alteratives include: Aloe, neem manjishtha, sandalwood, red clover, burdock, bayberry, black pepper, cinnamon, myrhh, and safflower.

Ama: Toxin produced by undigested food; the root cause of many diseases.

Amalaki: An Ayurvedic herb, same as Amla.

Amashaya: stomach.

Amavata: Ayurvedic term for arthritis, a disease caused by Vata and Ama.

Amla: An Ayurvedic herb with a sour taste.

Analgesic: Herbs that relieve pain, include camphor, chamomile, cinnamon, cloves, and echinacea.

Antacid: Neutralizes the acid produced by the stomach.

Anthelmintic: Kills and expels worms. (In Ayurveda, the term "worm" refers to all parasites.) Includes ajwan, cayenne, pepper, cloves, garlic, and golden seal.

Antiemetic: Relieves nausea and vomiting. Includes cloves, coriander, ginger, neem, and raspberry.

Antilithic: Help prevent the formation of stones in the kidneys and bladder.

Antiperiodic: Helps prevent the reappearance of a recurrent condition. Includes amalali, black peper, brihati, manjushtha, safflower, and sandalwood.

Antiphlogistic: Herb that counteracts inflammation. Includes barberry and white sandalwood.

Antipyretic: Fever reducing plant. Examples include aloe vera and neem.

Antiseptic: Prevents the growth of microorganisms. Includes aloe, gudmar, sandalwood, shatavari, shilajit, and turmeric.

Antispasmodic: Relieves muscle spasms. Herbs include ashwasabdha, basil, calamus, and guggul; licorice, myrrh, and sage for Vata and Kapha types and betony, brahmi, bhringaraj, jatamanshi, peppermint, sandalwood, and spearmint for Pitta types.

Antitussive: Prevents or relieves a cough.

Anurasa: A secondary flavor, a subordinate feeling.

Ap or Apa: Water.

Apana: One of the five types of Vata, which goes downward and is responsible for expulsion of feces, flatus, and urine.

Aperient: Mild laxative; includes rhubarb.

Arjuna: An Ayurvedic herb.

Artava dhatu: Female reproductive system.

Asana: Yoga posture.

Asatmya: Unwholesome, bad.

Ashoka: An Ayurvedic herb.

Asthi dhatu: Bone tissue.

Astringent: Drying to the skin or mucous membranes. Includes amalaki, arjuna, ashoka, cinnamon, jasmine, sandalwood, and yarrow.

Atisara: Diarrhea.

Ativisha: An Ayurvedic herb.

Aum: Sacred syllable.

Ayurveda: The science of life.

Bala: Strength.

Basmati rice: Long grained scented rice.

Bhasma: Burned gems or metals for ingesting.

Bhringgaraj: An Ayurvedic herb.

Bhutrina: Lemongrass.

Bibhitaki: An Ayurvedic herb.

Bij: Seed.

Bola: An Ayurvedic herb.

Brahmi: An Ayurvedic herb, gotu kola.

Brihati: An Ayurvedic herb.

Cardamom: Pungent spice.

Carminative: These herbs are rich in aromatic oils. They prevent gas from forming in the intestines. They are also good for the nervous system. Includes basil, chamomile, chrysanthemum, coriander, calamus, cardamom, cinnamon, and turmeric.

Chai: Tea.

Chakra: Energy center in the body.

Chaksu: Eye.

Chikitsa: Practice to Ayurvedic medicine to retain Dosha balance.

Chirayata: An Ayurvedic herb.

Cholagogue: Stimulates the flow of bile from the liver into the intestines. Includes bhringaraj, guduchi, licorice, and safflower.

Cilantro: Fresh coriander leaf.

Churna: Powder, usually herb powders.

Dal: Dried bean or lentil.

Danta roga: tooth disorders.

Daruharidra: An Ayurvedic herb (barberry).

Demulcent: Soothes mucus membranes. Includes barley, licorice, linseed, olive, and almond oils.

Dhanyak: An Ayurvedic herb (coriander).

Dhatu: Any of the main structural systems or tissues of the body.

Diaphoretic: Promotes circulation and perspiration (cooling). Includes angelica,cardamom, basil, ajwan, and ginger.

Discutient: Dissolves or causes something like a tumor or stone, to disappear.

Diuretic: Promotes the production of urine and healing of urinary organs.Herbs include ashwagandha, asparagus, barberry, cardamom, ginger, gotu kola, guduchi, licorice, punarnava, and sandalwood.

Dosha: Any of the three main principles of the body: Vata, Pitta or Kapha.

Drishti: Eye.

Ela: An Ayurvedic herb (cardamom).

Emollient: Soothes the skin.

Expectorant: Promotes the expulsion of mucus from the lungs and gas from the intestines. Includes ginger, calamus, cardamom, cinnamon, comfrey root, cloves, pippali, and licorice.

Gauraphal: An Ayurvedic herb (red raspberry).

Ghee: Clarified butter made by heating unsalted butter and removing the milk solids.

Ghrita: Ghee.

Gomedha: hessonite garnet.

Gudmar: An Ayurvedic herb.

Guggulu (Guggul): A resin from a small tree and medical herb. (Indian Bedellium).

Gulma: Abdominal tumors.

Guna: Any of the three qualities in the universe: sattva, rajas, or tamas.

Guru: Teacher; also the heavy quality of food.

Guti: Herbal pills.

Haritaki: An Ayurvedic herb.

Hemostatic: Stops bleeding.

Hridaya: Heart.

Hridroga: Heart disease.

Jala: Water, fluid.

Jara: Aging.

Jatamanshi: An Ayurvedic herb.

Jwara: fever.

Kakanasha: An Ayurvedic herb.

Kala: Season, time period.

Kamala roga: Jaundice.

Kantkari: An Ayurvedic herb.

Kapha: One of the three doshas – water. This is the energy that forms the body's structure.

Karma: Action, work.

Kashaya: Astringent.

Kapittaparni: Frankincense.

Karnapali roga: Ear flaps.

Karna-gata-roga-vijnaniya: Ear disorders.

Karpur: Camphor.

Kasa: Cough.

Kashaya: Astringent.

Katu: Pungent.

Katuka: An Ayurvedic herb.

Kumkum: An Ayurvedic herb (saffron).

Kundalini: Spiritual life force.

Kushtha: An Ayurvedic herb (kut).

Lavana: Salty.

Lepa: Paste or poultice.

Madhura: Sweet taste.

Majja: Bone marrow and nerve tissue.

Malas: Waste products excreted from the body.

Mamira: An Ayurvedic herb (gold thread).

Mamsa: Muscle tissue.

Manas: Mind.

Manda: Rice preparation.

Mantra: Sacred words or phrase.

Maricha: An Ayurvedic herb (black pepper).

Marma: Energy point on the skin.

Matsaya: Fish.

Meda: Fat or adipose tissue.

Murcha: Fainting.

Mutra: Urine.

Mutra ashmarai: Urinary stones.

Mutra ghata: Urine obstruction.

Mutra srota: Urinary channels.

Nada: Sound.

Nadi: Pulse, or nerve channel.

Nagkeshar: An Ayurvedic herb.

Nervine: Calms the nerves and reduces muscle spasms. Herbs include ashawgandhara, bala, basil, gudmar, jatamansi, and shankh pushpi.

Netra: Eye.

Netra basti: Medicated eye baths.

Nidra: Sleep.

Nirgundi: An Ayurvedic herb.

Odana: Boiled rice.

Ojas: Strength, vitality. The pure essence of all bodily tissues.

Pandu-roga: Anemia.

Panir (or Paneer): A type of cheese.

Peya: Rice gruel.

0Hot infusions.

Pippali: An Ayurvedic herb (long pepper) and relative of black pepper.

Pitta: One of the three doshas, corresponding to the principle of fire (the bile humor).

Prajna: Wisdom.

Prakriti: Cosmic creativity, the female principle.

Prana: Life energy, breath.

Pranayama: Breathing techniques.

Pritivi: Earth.

Punarnava: An Ayurvedic herb.

Purusha: Pure cosmic awareness.

Rajas: One of the gunas: dynamic energy.

Rakta: Blood.

Raktavaha srota: Circulatory channel.

Rasa: Plasma.

Rechaka: The exhaled breath.

Rechanaka: An Ayurvedic herb (raktam).

Resolvent: Reduces inflammation bye absorption.

Rishi: Ancient seer or wise person.

Roga: Disease.

Ruksa: Dry.

Rupa: Sign, symptom of disease.

Saffron: Golden yellow spice.

Samagni: Normal digestion.

Sankhya: School of Indian philosophy.

Sapta dhatus: Seven tissues.

Sariva: An Ayurvedic herb (sarsaparilla).

Sattva: Purity, clarity of perception.

Shamana: Palliation therapy.

Shankh pushpi: An Ayurvedic herb.

Shilajit: An Ayurvedic "herb," although it is actually a mineral.

Shira: Veins.

Shirsha: Head.

Shitali: Pranayama practice of cooling breath control.

Shukra: Male reproductive tissue.

Shunthi: Dry ginger.

Sialagogue: A substance that increases the production of saliva. Includes black pepper, chirayata, pippali, and licorice.

Snuhi: An Ayurvedic herb (vajra).

Srotas: Bodily channels.

Stimulants: Herbs that excite all the bodily organs. They include black pepper, cayenne, cinnamon, garlic and ginger.

Surya: Sun.

Surya Namaskar: Sun Salutation.

Swapna: Sleep.

Sweda: Sweat.

Tamas: One of the three gunas, darkness, inertia.

Tejbal: An Ayurvedic herb (tumburu).

Thailam: Any cooling, herbally infused oil.

Trayman: An Ayurvedic herb (wild violet).

Tiksna: Sharp, pungent, fiery.

Tonics: Restore tissues and nourish the body. Examples include almonds, dates, and honey.

Triguna: Three qualities of Nature.

Trikatu: Ayurvedic compound of ginger, black pepper, and pipalli.

Triphala: Ayurvedic compound made of amalaki, bibbitai and haritaki.

Trishna: Thirst.

Tulsi: Indian holy basil.

Twak: An Ayurvedic herb (cinnamon).

Udara roga: Abdominal disease.

Usna: Hot, sharp.

Uveitis: Inflammation of the iris and middle coat of the eyeball.

Vaidya: Ayurvedic practitioner.

Vamsha Lochana: An Ayurvedic herb (bamboo manna).

Vasaka: An Ayurvedic herb (vasak).

Vata: One of the three dosha, combing space and air elements.

Vidanga: An Ayurvedic herb.

Vrana: Wounds.

Yashtimadhu: An Ayurvedic herb (licorice).

Yoga: Union of the lower self with the higher self.